MiG-15 in action

By Hans-Heiri Stapfer
Color By Don Greer/Perry Manley
Illustrated By Perry Manley

Aircraft Number 116
squadron/signal publications

A MiG-15bis Fagot of the North Korean Peoples Air Force shoots down a Lockheed F-80C Shooting Star fighter-bomber over North Korea. When it was first introduced into combat in Korea, the MiG-15 came as a surprise to the United Nations air forces.

ISBN 0-89747-264-0

If you have any photographs of the aircraft, armor, soldiers or ships of any nation, particularly wartime snapshots, why not share them with us and help make Squadron/Signal's books all the more interesting and complete in the future. Any photograph sent to us will be copied and the original returned. The donor will be fully credited for any photos used. Please send them to:

Squadron/Signal Publications, Inc.
1115 Crowley Drive.
Carrollton, TX 75011-5010.

Dedication

This book is respectfully dedicated to anyone who beats my dieting record — 330 days on a demanding diet without losing a pound!

This book is also dedicated to all the people who share my strong distaste for light-beer, diet meals, mineral water, morning gymnastics, jogging, Diet-Coke, Nouvelle Cuisine, little food on large plates, empty glasses and nasty friends giving advice on how to lose weight.

Acknowledgements

Robert Gretzyngier
Robert Bock
Joe Merchant
George Punka
Tibor Sinka
Zdenek Hurt
Zdenek Titz
Jan Horn
Hans-Georg Volprich
Wilfried Kopenhagen
Kristina Donath
Martin Kyburz
Nigel A. Eastaway
Dave Hatherell
Larry Davis
Bob Bird
Manfred Griehl
Instytutu Lotnictwa
Shlomo Kleszcelski-Aloni
Chuck Stewart
Mariusz Zimny
Andrzej Morgala
Pilot's Pals
Odon Horvath
Andras Nagy
Jiri Vrany
Dusan Mikolas
Wolfgang Tamme
Hans-Joachim Mau
FOTAG
Alain Pelletier
Albert Violand
Simon Watson
Air Force Museum
Nicholas J. Waters III
Maxwell Research Center
Wolfgang Dressel
Hannu Valtonen
Wojciech Luczak
Helmut Kluger

Editor's Note

The MiG-15 is known to many as the Fagot. This name is not part of the Soviet designation for the aircraft, but is rather the name assigned to the aircraft by the Air Standards Coordinating Committee of NATO. The ASCC is made up of members from all the NATO nations and they decide the reporting names for new Soviet equipment.

The purpose of the NATO reporting name is to allow for rapid radio identification/reporting of Soviet aircraft types. The names are all designed to sound different so that they will not be confused, even under conditions of poor radio reception.

Single syllable names are used for propeller-driven aircraft, while multiple syllable names are used for jet-powered aircraft. The name also identifies the basic mission of the aircraft. Names beginning with B are bombers, names beginning with C denote transports, helicopters begin with H, and miscellaneous types (trainers, reconnaissance, etc) begin with M.

Fighter aircraft all have names beginning with F, therefore under the NATO system, the MiG-15 became the Fagot, denoting that it was a jet-powered fighter aircraft. Variants of the basic aircraft are usually identified by a suffix letter, with the second variant of the basic aircraft being identified as the Fagot B, etc. The two seat trainer variant of the MiG-15 was named the Midget, denoting it as a jet-powered trainer.

This MiG-15bis is probably one of the best known MiG-15s in existence. The aircraft is an ex-North Korean MiG-15 which was delivered by a defecting pilot. It was tested at Kadena Air Base on Okinawa and at Wright-Patterson AFB. The letters "TC" reportedly stood for Tom Collins, one of the MiG-15 test pilots.

U.S. AIR FORCE
7616

TC-616

Introduction

During November of 1950, United Nations fighter pilots over North Korea encountered a formidable swept-wing high performance jet fighter, which was quickly identified as the Soviet-built MiG-15. Almost overnight the name MiG became infamous in the West, as Sabres and MiG-15s clashed over "MiG Alley." The MiG-15 was the first jet fighter to be mass produced by the MiG Design Bureau and over the years the name MiG has become virtually synonymous with Soviet fighter.

MiG is actually an acronym made up of the last names of the two men heading the design bureau, Artjom Ivanovich Mikoyan and Mikhail Iosifovich Gurevich. The MiG Bureau was founded on 25 December 1939 at State Aircraft Factory Number 1, *Osoaviachim* at Frunse airfield on the outskirts of Moscow and during the Great Patriotic War (World War II) developed a number of fighters with impressive performance. None, other than the MiG-3, ever progressed beyond the prototype stage and MiG fighters were overshadowed by the designs of Yakovlev and Lavochkin.

Due the fact that the MiG bureau was downgraded to an experimental shop for new fighter designs, rather than a production center, the prototypes leaving State Aircraft Factory Number 1 at the end of the war were more advanced in design and performance than other Soviet aircraft. Mikoyan and Gurevich were more open minded toward innovative ideas than their more conservative rivals, Yakovlev and Lavochkin, who concentrated on improving existing fighter types.

After the war, the Soviet aviation industry sought to improve their designs to keep up with Western, in particular American and British, aircraft. The government had learned that their earlier policy of continuously improving existing aircraft was one of the reasons for the high losses in Soviet aircraft during the early stages of the Great Patriotic War. Producing modern, effective designs became even more important as the political climate between the Soviet Union and her former Allies (France, England and the United States) cooled.

During the Great Patriotic War, Lend-Lease aircraft, as well as captured German, Italian and Japanese designs were carefully tested and evaluated by the TsAGI (Central Aero-Hydrodynamics Institute) and most of the leading State Aircraft Factories. This was done to obtain information which could be used to improve Soviet aircraft. Most of the research done by the TsAGI was also made available to the leading design bureaus in the USSR.

A rich source of new information and research data were the captured German aircraft evaluated by the Test and Research Center of the Soviet Air Force at Ramenskoye. Even more important to the future of Soviet fighter development were the research documents found by advancing Soviet troops. The Soviet Union made good use of this information and German research data had a strong impact on future designs.

One of the most advanced designs captured was the Ta-183 designed by Kurt Tank. It was a swept wing, single engined jet fighter with a T tail. It had an estimated speed of 590 mph and a service ceiling of 47,000 feet. Built mainly of wood, the first prototype was scheduled to fly during August of 1945 and research had continued until May of 1945 when Allied troops captured the facilities.

The most outstanding feature of the Ta-183 design was its wing. Based on research by Professors Goethert and Ruden on the aerodynamics of swept wings, the Ta-183 featured a wing with very little thickness and a 35 degree sweep.

During January of 1946, long before the first Soviet jet powered aircraft flew, the State Defense Committee issued a specification for an advanced high altitude day interceptor fighter with a top speed of Mach 0.9 and a service ceiling of over 30,000 feet. The Design Bureaus of Yakovlev, Lavochkin and MiG were all given the specification. It was intended that all three design bureaus would work closely with the TsAGI, since many captured German reports had been evaluated there.

When the swept wing fighter project was launched at the MiG Design Bureau, the program received the Project designation S for *Strelowidnostji* (Swept). Before the first drawings were done on Project S, a team of academics, led by Professors Savizkj and Sudez, carefully analyzed the aerodynamics of the swept wing. This program also included a number of German specialists; however, none of the Germans were later involved on Project S. The program was a joint venture between MiG and the TsAGI to guarantee the stability of the swept back wing at high speeds during maneuvers. The goal was to achieve the best possible angle of sweep and the proper degree of wing anhedral.

This program proved to be rather long and difficult. Models of the swept wing fighter were tested at the TsAGI wind tunnel, which was modernized with German equipment and know-how. The leading Soviet aeronautical engineers engaged on the wing study program were S.A. Khristianovich, G.P. Svishchev, J.M. Serebrisky and W.W. Streminsky.

Another problem facing MiG was finding a suitable engine to power the fighter. During 1946, the most powerful jet engine available to MiG was the RD-10, a copy of the German Junkers Jumo 004. It was anticipated, however, that a progressive development of the engine, producing twice the thrust, would be available for flight testing the following year. The engine was not ready, however, and this led to further delays in the Project S program.

Initially, it was estimated that the prototype would require an axial flow engine of 6,000 pounds thrust. When it became evident that engines of this power output would not be available in the Soviet Union for years, every effort was made to reduce the weight of the aircraft to a maximum of 10,000 pounds.

The weight reduction program was not the only problem the MiG engineers had to contend with. When the decision was made to use the British manufactured Rolls-Royce Nene power plant, the change from an axial flow to a centrifugal flow power plant, with its greater diameter, led to a major redesign of the Project S fuselage and resulted in still further delays. Had the British not agreed to sell the Nene to the Soviet Union, Project S would have had suffered further delays.

The general aerodynamic layout of the MiG-15 was influenced by research done on the Focke Wulf Ta-183 project. This 1/10 scale wind tunnel model reveals some of the features adopted by the Soviets for their early jet fighters developed by both MiG and Lavochkin. (Manfred Griehl via Joachim Dressel)

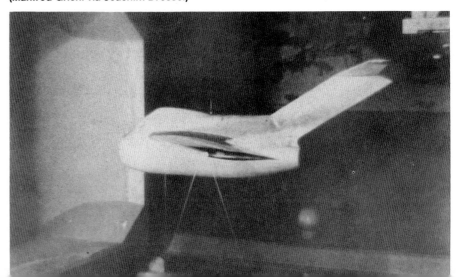

Between 1946 and 1947, some thirty Rolls Royce Derwent Mark V and twenty-five Rolls-Royce Nene Mark I engines were imported by the Soviet Union, over the strong opposition of both the Royal Air Force and the Defense Ministry. Shortly after their arrival in the Soviet Union, the power plants were given to several design bureaus, including MiG, Lavochkin and Iljushin, while one of the Nenes served as a pattern engine for an unlicensed copy.

During early 1947, work on the Project S prototype began at State Aircraft Factory 1 at Frunse airfield. The first prototype received the internal MiG designation S-01, while the Air Force had allocated the designation I-310 to the prototype (when the aircraft was cleared for production, the service designation MiG-15 was assigned).

Shortly after completion, the prototype was taken to Ramenskoye airfield where the factory tests began. The factory flight tests were conducted under the leadership of Konstantine Pavlovich Kovaljewskij. The S-01 prototype flew for the first time on 30 December 1947 with Viktor Nikolayevich Yuganov at the controls. The prototype had an armament of a single NS-37 37MM and two NS-23 23MM cannons and was powered by an original Rolls-Royce Nene power plant.

The weather in December, which had delayed the first flight of the S-01 prototype, presented a continuing problem. Since it was evident that the weather would not clear up during the Winter months, and flight testing had to be carried out in order to refine the aircraft for the upcoming State Acceptance trials, Mikoyan decided to dismantle the prototype and ship it via rail to the southern USSR, where conditions were much more favorable for testing.

The flight test revealed a number of shortcomings with the prototype. One major engineering modification resulting from the early testing was a reduction in the tail pipe of about one foot. Other modifications included a change in the sweep of the tailplane and a small modification to the wing trailing edge. One of the more serious shortcomings on the prototype was a tendency to stall and spin during a tight turn. Additionally, the aircraft had poor handling at high angles of attack and snaked as the speed rose above Mach 0.88.

While the S-01 prototype was retained for further factory tests, the second prototype (S-02) was allocated to the LII-GA (Flight Experimental Institute of Civil Aviation) on 27 May 1948. S-02 was soon followed by the third prototype (S-03) which was allocated to the LII-GA on 5 July 1948. Besides test pilot V.N. Yuganov, MiG test pilots I.T. Ivashchenko and S. N. Anokhin were also involved in the factory flight testing of the prototypes, while the State Acceptance trials were run by COLs Grigori Sedov, Jurij Antipov and Andrej G. Kochetkov.

Comparison evaluations conducted by the NII-VVS-RKKA (Science and Experimental Institute of the Soviet Air Force) at Ramenskoye revealed that the Lavochkin 174 had better flying characteristics at high speeds, while the MiG prototypes were superior in armament and climbing performance. Operations under field conditions clearly showed that the MiG had better serviceability and was easier to maintain. The State Acceptance trials with LII-GA and NII-VVS-RKKA lasted until late 1948 as shortcomings found by both institutions were resolved on the prototypes.

One of the problems detected during operational trials was that during firing of the inboard 23MM cannon, gun gases were ingested into the intake, causing compressor stalls in the Rolls-Royce Nene. A redesign of the gun mount solved this problem.

There were a number of small differences between the S-01 and S-02. The S-01 had a small auxiliary frame on the canopy. The S-02 had an antenna fairing on top of the fuselage, the tail pipe was slightly redesigned and it was equipped with speed brakes on the rear fuselage. The inner main wheel doors of the S-01 only opened during the cycling of the landing gear and were closed when the aircraft was on the ground. On the S-02 the doors were open when the aircraft was on ground.

During late 1948, the prototypes were cleared for mass production at State Aircraft Factory 1 and other production plants under the service designation MiG-15. The MiG-15 was clearly a great achievement for the Soviet Union. In only one decade the Soviet Air Force had gone from the biplane Polikarpov I-153 to the forefront of the jet era, second only to the United States in advanced jet fighter design!

The Project S prototype, S-01, flew for the first time on 30 December 1947 with MiG test pilot Viktor Nikolayevich Yuganov at the controls. The aircraft was powered by a Rolls-Royce Nene engine and was not equipped with a gun camera.

The S-02 was the second prototype built and tested. The aircraft was delivered for State acceptance trials on 27 May 1948. It differed from the first prototype in that it had a radio antenna fairing on the fuselage spine and the inboard main wheel doors remained down when the aircraft was on the ground (they retracted on the S-01).

Development

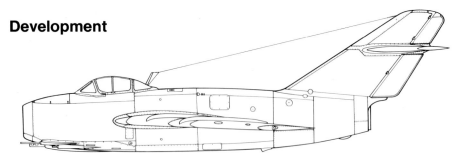

I-310 (S-01)
MiG-15 Prototype

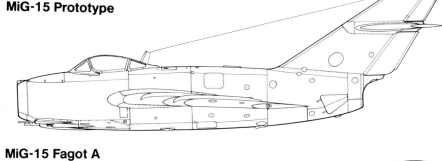

MiG-15 Fagot A

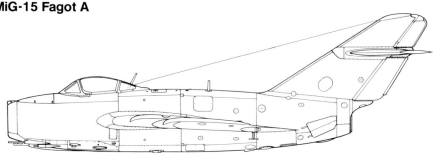

MiG-15bis Fagot B (Late)

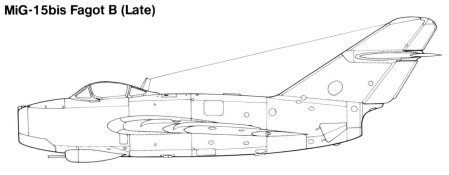

MiG-15U (SU)

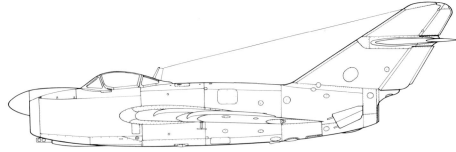

MiG-15P (SP-1)

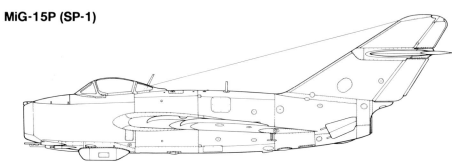

MiG-15bis R

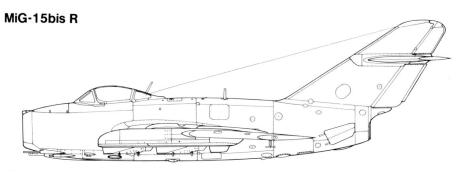

MiG-15 ISh

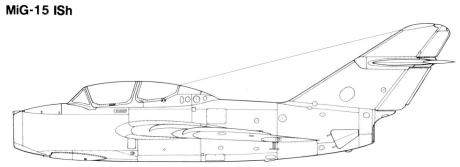

MiG-15 UTI

MiG-15 Fagot A

The first production MiG-15 made its maiden flight on 30 December 1948, exactly a year after the first flight of the project S prototype. Once again, MiG test pilot Viktor N. Yuganov made the first flight.

The production MiG-15 differed from the S-01 prototype in a number of ways. The canopy framing was revised and the center band was deleted. An S-13 gun camera was mounted in a fairing above the air intake. The rudder was enlarged slightly with a long trim tab being added to the trailing edge. The jet tail pipe was shortened and the fuselage contour above the tail pipe was changed slightly. A radio antenna fairing was added to the fuselage spine and an oval access panel was added to the fin.

Speed brakes were installed on the fuselage sides just in front of the tail pipe. These speed brakes opened out and slightly down and were operated by hydraulic jacks via an electrical selector switch. The brakes could be operated either from the control stick (for short periods), or they could be selected open or closed by a two-position toggle switch on the port side console directly under the radio controls. Adjacent to this switch was a Green light that indicated the position of the speed brakes (on when the speed brakes are open).

The production MiG-15 was an all-metal stressed-skin monoplane jet fighter with a 35 degree swept wing. The wing featured powered ailerons, which were internally balanced and modified Fowler type flaps on the wing trailing edge. The flaps were multi-position, with one setting for take off (20 degrees) and another for landing (55 degrees). The flaps operated hydraulically and had mechanical up-locks which were also operated hydraulically. In an emergency, the flaps could be extended by an emergency pneumatic system. There is a mechanical indicator located on the port wing between the air flow wing fences. This indicator consisted of a rod approximately two inches long painted in Black and White stripes which extended above the wing surface when the flaps were down. The horizontal tail was swept 40 degrees with separate elevators and trim tabs.

First tests in front line evaluation units showed that the aircraft suffered from buffeting when flying at the maximum allowable speed of 0.92 Mach. This was considered

This early production MiG-15 was used by the NII-VVS to test the use of RATO equipment. The rocket pods were carried under the wings on the standard bomb rack. The MiG-15 did not carry a tactical number but was painted with Yellow bands on the fin below the stabilizer.

This Soviet-built MiG-15 Fagot A, coded Black ME-36, of the Czech Air Force made a belly landing on a field in Bohemia. Salvage crews have already placed air-bags under the wings to raise the aircraft so the landing gear can be lowered and the aircraft towed off.

quite dangerous and, therefore, it was decided to decrease maximum speed allowed in operational units from 0.92 Mach to 0.88 Mach. The reason for the buffeting was that production tolerances of the first production aircraft were inaccurate; i.e., the wing profile had dimensions of about 4mm off of what it should have been. When the craftsmanship on the production line was improved to the desired standard, the MiG-15 was again cleared for a top speed of Mach 0.92.

The MiG-15 was equipped with a tricycle landing gear with the nose gear retracting into a well under the engine air ducting and the main landing gear retracting inward into wells between the wing spars. Mechanical indicators were installed to show the pilot that the landing gear was in the down position. The nose gear indicator was located on the port upper nose and was visible through the left hand corner of the windscreen. The main wheel indicator protruded from each wing when the main wheels are down. The wheel brakes were pneumatically operated by an air bottle which also served as the emergency landing gear blow down system. The brakes are activated by a lever positioned on the upper left side of the control stick.

The MiG-15 was powered by the 5,000 lbst RD-45 turbojet engine, a copy of the Rolls-Royce Nene. While the MiG-15 prototypes were being built, the Klimov Design Bureau at State Factory Number 117 was engaged in copying the Nene power plant. An original British engine was stripped and studied by the the design staff, which began the production drawings of the new engine at Klimov's main design office in Leningrad.

On 30 October 1947, most of the staff involved in the Nene project were transferred to the vast production plant at Zavod 45 in Moscow. The head of the Klimov design bureau was Vladimir Yakovlevich Klimov, who had developed the most successful engine produced in the USSR during WW II, the VK-105 (based on a French design). Copying the British Nene engine was a difficult undertaking since every item in the power plant had to be checked for specification, function, manufacturing process, tolerance, material and fit. Finally all this information had to be translated to Soviet equivalents with metric gauges instead of the British inch gauges. The Soviet Nene copy was designated the RD-45, after the Moscow factory designation. The RD-45 was also used in the La-15 and Il-28 bomber. There were a number of different variants of the RD-45, although most of the changes were detail changes such as different fittings to allow installation of the engine on various aircraft types. The RD-45F was an improved engine with water injection. One major shortcoming common to early RD-45 engines was the short time between overhauls and high fuel consumption. These faults were corrected on the RD-45F.

Avionics installed in the MiG-15 included an RPK-10M radio compass, a DGMK-3 direction finder and an RSI-6K radio, which was replaced by an RSI-6M-1 radio on late production aircraft. Early MiG-15s lacked an IFF system, radio altimeter, and radio marker beacon receiver when they left the factory. During its operational life, however, a number of MiG-15s were upgraded by the installation of an SRU-O IFF system with its blade antenna being mounted on top of the fuselage and an RV-2 radio altimeter with the T antennas being mounted under each wing.

There were a number of detail changes made to the MiG-15 during its production life (late 1948 to early 1950) before the aircraft was phased out in favor of the improved MiG-15bis.

The empty weight of the MiG-15 varied between production batches, as detail changes were introduced based on feed back from operational units. One improvement was an aileron boost system (Type BU-1U), another feature on late production aircraft was an automatic system for programming the engine starting cycle, permitting jet engine starts on the ground using the aircraft's internal battery system. This was done to reduce scramble time and to reduce the number of battery carts needed in each unit. Some late production aircraft had the port side inboard wing fence modified with a curved cut out. This was done to give the pilot an improved view of the flap indicator rod.

The armament of the MiG-15 consisted of two NS-23 23MM cannons on the port side of the nose with a single NS-37 37MM cannon mounted on the starboard side. All three guns were carried on an internal platform, which could be lowered by a hand crank after the cannon barrel fairings were removed. This simple and effective system allowed the guns to be easily and quickly rearmed and maintained in the field.

The NS-23 was developed by A. Nudelman and A. Suranow during 1945. It weighed 81.5 pounds, had a muzzle velocity of 2,263 feet per second and a rate of fire of 550 rounds per minute with eighty rounds per gun. The NS-37 had become operational during 1942. It weighed 330 pounds, had a muzzle velocity of 2,952 feet per second and a rate of fire of 250 rounds per minute with forty rounds being carried. The MiG-15 was equipped with an ASP-1B gun sight, which was later replaced by an ASP-1N gun sight on late production aircraft. All MiG-15s were equipped with a Type S-13 gun camera and an EKSR-46 flare dispenser was fitted on the starboard side of the tail. This was used to fire colored signal flares. The MiG-15 was equipped with a BDK-2-48MIG bomb rack under the wing to carry either bombs or either 66 (250 liter) or 79 (300 liter) gallon drop tanks. If the MiG-15 was flown without ammunition it was necessary to ballast the nose compartment to maintain the proper center of gravity.

Throughout the early production cycles, a lack of quality control and poor craftsmanship was a serious problem. Quite often manufacturing tolerances were exceeded but there was no supervisor checking the parts for quality. The only goal was to meet the "Five Year Plan," and this plan only called for certain production numbers, but did not mention a word about quality. As a result the handling qualities of MiG-15s within the same production block, and even on aircraft which left the factory one after the other were totally different. Some MiG-15s handled easily, while others were tricky to fly. Regardless of these problems, MiG-15s were allocated to combat units.

The problem with poor craftsmanship and lack of quality control on the production lines did not only affect the MiG-OKB; it was a typical Communist problem which was also found in other production plants manufacturing other highly sophisticated aircraft, such as the La-15 and Il-28.

Six months after the first production aircraft rolled off the assembly line, the aircraft was introduced to the public at the Soviet Aviation Day air show held at Tushino during July of 1948 (one of the prototypes was shown). After this show, the aircraft was used at

A pilot and ground crewman inspect the cannon muzzles of the NS-23 and NS-37 cannons and the nose wheel doors of Red 369, a MiG-15 of the Romanian Air Force. The aircraft is equipped with 66 gallon (250 liter) slipper drop tanks under the wings. The aircraft in the background is a Lisunov Li-2, a Soviet copy of the Douglas C-47.

Fuselage Development

S-01 Prototype

Narrow Rudder

Long Tail Pipe

No Speed Brake

MiG-15 Fagot A

Gun Camera Fairing

Revised Canopy Framing

Radio Antenna

Added Access Panel

Wider Rudder

Trim Tab

Recontoured Fuselage

Shortened Tail Pipe

Speed Brake

shows in increasing numbers: forty-five appeared in the 1949 May Day fly-over, fifty-two took part in an air show on 17 July and ninety participated in an air show on 7 November 1949. The largest number observed at any one time was 139. These aircraft participated in the 1950 May Day air show and fly-over.

Once NATO had identified the MiG-15 as an operational fighter, it assigned the reporting name Fagot to the MiG-15. (Initially, for a short period, the aircraft was named Falcon) The MiG-15 received various nicknames in service with both the Soviet and other countries. It was called *Samoljot-Soldat* (aircraft of the soldier) in Soviet service and *Jaguar* by the Hungarians.

MiG-15PB

Trials with early production MiG-15s clearly showed that the aircraft had insufficient range on its internal fuel supply. As a result the MiG-OKB developed a new variant which was able to carry a 66 gallon (250 liter) slipper type drop tank under each wing on the bomb rack. The MiG-15PB (*Podvyesnije Baki* - Belly Tank) was identical to standard MiG-15s apart from the additional internal equipment, such as pumps and fuel lines for the fuel transfer system. The tanks could be jettisoned when empty or before an engagement. Since the trials of this new variant were very successful, the modification was standardized and introduced on the production line. With the tanks now standard equipment, the PB designation was deleted and the aircraft simply called MiG-15s.

This Romanian MiG-15 Fagot A was used in a movie and painted in a special color scheme. The Blue arrow on the fuselage and tactical number were in the same shade of Blue as the national insignia marking. The Blue tactical number was in sharp contrast with normal Romanian practice of using Red tactical numbers on fighter aircraft.

Romanian ground crew run to their MiG-15 at Deveselu Airfield during 1962. Red 306 has been modified with an SRU-0 IFF blade antenna on the fuselage spine and an RV-2 radio altimeter antenna on the wing root.

A MiG-15 taxies out from the flight line at Deveselu Airfield for a sortie during the Summer of 1962. All the aircraft in the lineup have been modified with an SRU-0 IFF blade antenna mounted behind the radio antenna fairing on the fuselage spine. Some of the aircraft have the Red three digit tactical number outlined in White, while others are outlined in Black.

Romanian pilots receive last minute instructions prior to starting a mission, while ground crewmen conduct preflight inspections of their MiG-15s. Some of the maintenance inscriptions have been changed from Russian to Romanian. The national markings, carried on the rear fuselage and vertical fin, was unusual for a WARSAW Pact country. This marking was used between 1949 and 1985, and the Red star was always outlined in White and Blue.

Romanian ground crews remove the protective covers from a MiG-15 Fagot A, Red 306, before a mission. The muzzles for the NS-23 and NS-37 cannons are also covered. The air intake cover is Red with the aircraft tactical number on it in White. The two piece gun blast panel is standard for the Fagot A and was used on early production MiG-15bis fighters.

MiG-15S

The MiG-15S (S for *Soprovozdenije*, Escort) was an escort fighter variant of the MiG-15 Fagot A. The only difference between the MiG-15 and MiG-15S was the provision for carrying two 66 gallon (250 liter), 79 gallon (300 liter) or 105 gallon (400 liter) slipper type drop tanks and 158.5 gallon (600 liter) underwing style tanks on the standard underwing bomb racks. When this provision was adopted for all production MiG-15s the designation MiG-15S was dropped.

MiG-15SV

The MiG-15SV (SV for Soprovozdenije Vysoto, High Altitude Escort) was developed as a high altitude escort fighter based on the standard MiG-15. The aircraft was equipped with underwing tanks and, to reduce weight, the armament was changed. The aircraft was equipped with the more advanced NR-23 23MM cannon in place of the NS-23 cannon usually carried (the 37MM cannon was retained). The NR-23 became the standard weapon used on the later MiG-15bis variants, and could be easily identified by the shorter gun fairings and a blistered shell ejection ports.

Late in their service career, Romanian MiG-15 were used in the ground attack role and camouflaged in Earth Brown and Olive Drab uppersurfaces, with Light Blue undersurfaces. The Red tactical number was outlined in White and the national insignia was applied to the vertical fin and both top and bottom of the wing.

Soviet built MiG-15s of 1 PLM *Warszawa* on the ramp at their home base of Minsk-Mazowiecki. The aircraft in the foreground has a two digit tactical number, while the next Fagot A carries a single digit tactical number (both in Red). The MiG-15 was shown to the Polish public for the first time on 26 August 1951 at an air show over Okecie, Warsaw's International Airport.

Standard Drop Tanks

66 Gallon (250 Liter) Slipper Tank

Filler Cap

79 Gallon (300 Liter) Slipper Tank

105 Gallon (400 Liter) Underwing Tank

Sway Brace

Pylon

Fins

This was one of the first MiG-15 fighters delivered to Poland during 1951. The aircraft were shipped dismantled in crates and reassembled in Poland. The first unit re-equip with the MiG-15 was 1 PLM (*Pulk Lotnictwa Mysliwskiego*, Fighter Regiment) based at Minsk-Mazowiecki. Single digit Red tactical numbers were only in use for a short time.

11

During the 1960s a number of MiG-15s were used by the Polish State Railway to clean the tracks of ice and snow. The rear fuselage and wings were removed and the engine was operated from the cockpit.

Obsolete MiG-15s were used for fire fighting training exercises, such as this Polish Air Force MiG-15. The aircraft was anchored on concrete pads and flares were used to simulate an actual fire. All usable equipment and armament has been removed from the aircraft.

The MiG-15 was known as the *Jaguar* in Hungarian Air Force service. This aircraft has a Red tactical number (outlined in White) and Red lower fuselage and underwing surfaces. When the MiG-15 was superseded by the later MiG-15bis, the *Jaguars* were returned to the USSR.

Oversize Drop Tank

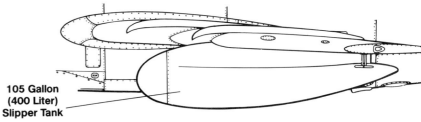

105 Gallon (400 Liter) Slipper Tank

The MiG-15S was developed as an escort fighter and carried oversized 105 gallon (400 liter) slipper tanks. These tanks were considerably larger than the standard 66 gallon (250 liter) or 79 gallon (300 liter) slipper tanks. This trials aircraft carried no tactical number during testing carried out by the NII-VVS.

MiG-15U (Project SU)

One of several projects aimed at providing the MiG-15 with a ground attack capacity was the MiG-15U (Project SU). This aircraft was to be armed with two cannons with swiveling barrels mounted in large fairings under the nose. The designation SU reflected this armament (S for MiG-15 project and U for *Ustanovka*, weapon-swiveling device). Its service designation was MiG-15U.

The MiG-15U was based on a standard MiG-15 Fagot A. The original armament was deleted and replaced by two NR-30 30MM cannons which were mounted, along with their ammunition, in rounded fairings under the nose. The guns were capable of movement through a vertical arc of minus 55 degrees to plus 5 degrees. The standard two piece gun blast panel was replaced by an enlarged single piece blast panel to protect the aircraft skinning from the effects of the gun muzzle blast.

The NR-30 was a new weapon developed by A.A. Nudelman and A. Richter. The gun became operational with the Soviet Air Force during 1954 and was the standard gun used on the MiG-19S Farmer and the MiG-21F-13 Fishbed. The weapon was based on the same principles as the reliable NR-23. It weighed 145.5 pounds (66 kg), had a muzzle velocity of 2,559 feet per second and a rate of fire of 900 rounds per minute.

After completing factory testing, the aircraft was transferred to the *NIIVVSRKKA* (Science and Experimental Institute of the Air Force) at Ramenskoye for weapon trials. There was only one MiG-15U built, which was evaluated with the tactical number "Red 935." The results of the weapons trials were far from what the Air Force had expected and the entire project was cancelled. Since NATO was not aware of the project, no NATO reporting name was ever given to the MiG-15U.

Armament

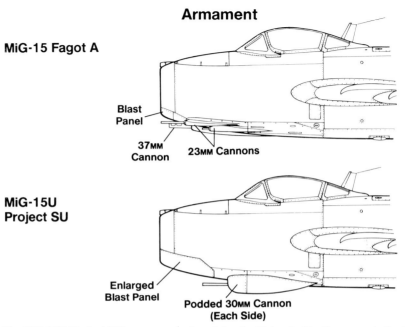

MiG-15 Fagot A

Blast Panel

37MM Cannon

23MM Cannons

MiG-15U Project SU

Enlarged Blast Panel

Podded 30MM Cannon (Each Side)

The MiG-15U (Project SU) was an experimental variant intended for the ground attack role. It was armed with two NR-30 30MM cannons in large gondolas behind the nose wheel bay and an enlarged gun blast panel. Red 935 was evaluated by the NIIVVSRKKA at Ramenskoye.

SP-1

The SP-1 became the MiG OKB's first all weather interceptor, equipped with an air intercept radar system. The development of the SP-1 (P for *Perekhvachik*, Interceptor) was based on a requirement issued by Marshall Govorov of the Air Defense Forces (PVO) during 1949. The specification called for a fighter that was capable of action under all weather conditions and at night. The interceptor was to be capable to detecting a target without visual contact, then intercepting and destroying it.

The airborne intercept radar system was called *Korshun* (Vulture) and was developed by a team under the leadership of Andrjeja Slepushkin. The system was based on a single antenna which performed both search and tracking functions. The antenna was operated manually for tracking the target.

The *Korshun* system was installed in a MiG-15bis Fagot B with a heavily modified nose section. To make room for the radar system and to reduce the aircraft's weight, the standard MiG-15 three gun armament was reduced to a single NS-37 cannon with forty-five rounds of ammunition mounted on the starboard side of the nose. The S-13 gun camera was relocated from the top of the air intake to the port side of the nose. The two piece nosewheel doors were relocated with a larger single piece nosewheel door, hinged to open to port. The RV-2 radio altimeter antennas were relocated to a position on the underside of the wing outboard of the wing fences. The SP-1 also had the radio antenna fairing on the fuselage upper surfaces deleted.

The weight of the radar changed the aircraft's center of gravity and ballast had to be added to compensate for this problem. There was a problem in heating the system at high altitudes and finding a reliable material for covering the radome was another difficult task.

The radar search/track antenna was mounted on the air intake splitter duct and only reduced the airflow by about twenty percent. This type of mounting was also used on later radar equipped MiGs including the MiG-17PF and MiG-19PM.

The SP-1 proved to be unsuccessful and only a single prototype was built. As an experimental test aircraft, the SP-1 provided the MiG-OKB with useful data on radar equipped all-weather fighters and later led to other more successful fighters.

The SP-1 was an attempt by the MIG-OKB to develop a radar equipped all weather interceptor variant of the MiG-15. Development work on the aircraft began during 1949 and it was basically a MiG-15 airframe fitted with the *Korshun* (Vulture) radar system.

Nose Development

MiG-15bis

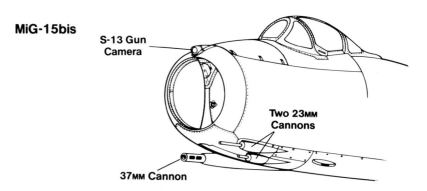

S-13 Gun Camera

Two 23MM Cannons

37MM Cannon

Only one SP-1 prototype was constructed and tested. The aircraft was armed with a single NS-37 cannon on the starboard side of the nose, with the standard two port side NS-23 cannons being deleted to save weight.

SP-1

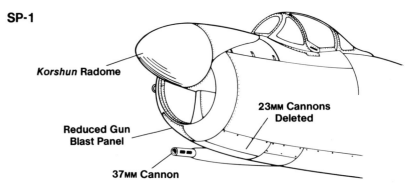

Korshun Radome

23MM Cannons Deleted

Reduced Gun Blast Panel

37MM Cannon

SP-5

The SP-5 was a parallel development to the *Korshun* equipped SP-1 differing in the radar system, nose shape and armament. The SP-5 was equipped with the *Izumrud* (Smaragd) radar system developed by a team under the leadership of Viktor Tikhomirov. This radar used two antennas, one for search and another for track. This had the advantage that the tracking of a target was done automatically rather than manually as with the *Korshun* system.

The lip fairing above the air intake housed the RP-1 search antenna under a plastic covering. The radar was able to pick up targets at twelve kilometers (7.45 miles) range and when the target was within two kilometers (1.24 miles) it switched automatically from search to track. The tracking antenna was fitted in the intake splitter which occupied the middle of the air intake. In addition to the radar screen, there were two colored lights in the cockpit: a Green light told the pilot when the target was within 3,000 meters and, if the pilot approached closer than 500 meters, a Red lamp came on warning that the target was too close. The radar was used in conjunction with the ASP optical gunsight.

Armament included two NR-23 cannons mounted on either side of the nose above the nosewheel doors. The gun blast panel on the starboard side was slightly larger than the panel on the port side. The aircraft was equipped with a recording camera mounted on top of the forward canopy frame, as well as the standard S-13 gun camera which was relocated to the starboard side of the nose.

The SP-5 flew for the first time during 1950 and the aircraft soon followed a small production batch which carried the service designation MiG-15P (P, *Perekhvachik*, Interceptor).

The SP-5 was equipped with an RP-1 *Izumrud-1* (Emerald) radar system. The aircraft carried a special test camera mounted above the forward canopy frame. The aircraft was armed with a single a NR-23 cannon on each side of the nose above the nose wheel door.

Radar Installation

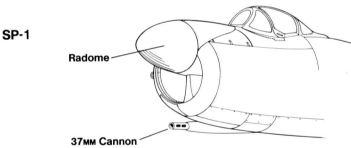

SP-1

Radome

37мм Cannon

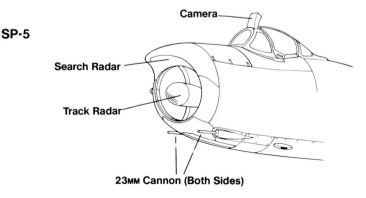

SP-5

Camera

Search Radar

Track Radar

23мм Cannon (Both Sides)

The SP-5 carried the RP-1 *Izumrud-1* radar housed in an extended lip above the air intake. The lip was painted Gloss Light Blue, while the radome was White. The installation of the radar caused the S-13 gun camera to be repositioned to the port side of the intake.

MiG-15bis Fagot B (Project SD)

During 1949, MiG engineers began work on an improved variant of the MiG-15 to be powered by a 5,950 lbst VK-1 power plant. This aircraft was developed under the MiG-OKB project code SD.

The power plant was developed by the Vladimir Y. Klimov design bureau. During 1946, the OKB had started studies aimed at improving the performance and reliability of the Rolls-Royce Nene. These studies resulted in the VK-1 power plant (the VK designation was assigned in honor of the chief designer, Vladimir Klimov). The engine was essentially an improved Nene that increased available thrust from 5,000 lbst to 5,950 lbst without changing the overall diameter of the power plant. The engine featured enlarged combustion chambers, turbine blades and tail pipe.

In November of 1948, the VK-1 passed the state acceptance trials and was cleared for production at State Factory 45 in Moscow. It was followed by the improved VK-1A. The engine was the basis for the MiG-OKB SD project. Although similar to a late production MiG-15, the SD prototype differed from the basic MiG-15 Fagot A in a number of ways.

To handle the increased power and fuel demands of the VK-1, the SD aircraft had the internal fuel capacity raised from 330 gallons (1,250 liters) on the Fagot A to 372 gallons (1,410 liters) on the SD aircraft. The larger fuselage fuel tank occupied the lower half of the fuselage and had a capacity of 42 gallons (160 liters).

There were a number of different styles of wing tanks used on the SD aircraft including a 66 gallon (250 liters) slipper tank, a 79 gallon (300 liter) slipper tank, a 105 gallon (400 liters) slipper tank and a 158.5 gallon (600 liters) underwing tank. The use of the 158.5 gallon (600 liters) tanks was restricted to bases with long hard surface runways because of the increased takeoff run required when using the large tanks. Landings with two full 158.5 gallon tanks was forbidden because of their weight.

The SD prototype flew for the first time in September 1949, with test pilot Antipov at the controls. After a series of successful trials, the aircraft was ordered into production under the service designation MiG-15bis, with actual series production beginning during 1950. As with the earlier MiG-15 there were differences in equipment and detail changes between production blocks as improvements were progressively introduced into the MiG-15bis production line. As a result, empty weight and performance were different depending on the production batch and the production plant.

The first production MiG-15bis fighters off the assembly line at State Aircraft Factory Number One at Frunze airfield were quite similar to the last production batches of MiG-15s with the exception of the introduction of an enlarged speed brake on the MiG-15bis. Additionally, thanks to an ongoing weight reduction program, the MiG-15bis weighed some 198 pounds less than a MiG-15.

Besides the speed brake, the MiG-15bis differed from the MiG-15 in having the radio antenna fairing on top of the fuselage deleted, a number of repositioned access panels on the tail, the tail bumper was slightly enlarged and was moved further back on the underside of the fuselage.

Most MiG-15bis fighters were equipped with the RV-2 radio altimeter. Initially, the T shaped antennas were placed on the underside of the wingtip (port side) and above the NS-37 cannon fairing (starboard side). After a short period, the starboard antenna was repositioned to a position on the underside of the wing just inboard of the first wing fence.

Although some early MiG-15bis fighters lacked the SRU-O IFF blade antenna on the fuselage spine, most production MiG-15bis aircraft carried this antenna (which was also retrofitted on a number of earlier aircraft). The EKSR-46 flare dispenser was relocated from under the starboard rear fuselage to a position on the upper starboard fuselage near the tail.

There were a number of changes in the avionics carried in the MiG-15bis. The earlier RSI-6M-1 radio was replaced by an improved R-800 radio. Although some early production MiG-15bis fighters had an RPKO-10M radio compass, this was quickly replaced by an ARK-5 radio compass on the majority of MiG-15bis production blocks. All MiG-15s and a number of early MiG-15bis aircraft had the radio antenna lead running from the tail directly to the radio aerial mast, while on most MiG-15bis aircraft the HF antenna cable connected to a small button lead-in just in front of the aerial mast.

During mid-1951, a major change in the armament system was introduced on the MiG-15bis production line. Early batches of the MiG-15bis had been equipped with the same armament as the MiG-15. After mid-1951, the MiG-15bis was armed with the two NR-23 cannons (instead of NS-23 cannons) on the port fuselage side and a single N-37 cannon on the starboard side.

Externally the NR-23 could be identified by the shorter gun fairings over the guns and the blistered shell ejection ports behind the guns. The NR-23 had an improved ammunition feed system, and a higher rate of fire (850 rounds per minute instead of 550 rpm). Although it used the same ammunition as the earlier NS-23, the NR-23 had a muzzle velocity of 2,263 feet per second, a rate of fire of 400 rounds per minute and an ammunition capacity of forty-five rounds (five rounds more than on the NS-23).

While early aircraft were equipped with the ASP-1N gunsight, it was replaced by the ASP-3N gunsight on later production MiG-15bis fighters. The cockpit armament controls were simple selection switches. The guns could be fired as follows: all guns, N-37 gun only (with or without camera), or both NR-23 guns only (with or without camera). Additionally, by charging only one NR-23, it is possible to fire one NR-23 or one NR-23 and the N-37. Soviet armament experts estimated that it would require only two N-37 or eight NR-23 hits to shoot down a B-29, B-50, or B-36. A single N-37 or one/two NR-23 hits were enough to destroy aircraft such as the F-80, F-84 or F-86.

The first MiG-15bis (SD) prototype during acceptance trials with the NII-VVS. The MIG-15bis/SD prototype retained the Fagot A type radio antenna fairing on the fuselage spine and small speed brakes. The SD prototype had NR-23 cannons installed (short cannon fairings and blistered shell ejection ports) while early production MiG-15bis fighters retained the earlier NS-23 guns.

Initial production blocks of the MiG-15bis, as well as all MiG-15s, had the landing light mounted in the upper portion of the air intake splitter. Later production MiG-15bis aircraft had the light repositioned to the underside of the port wing root with the intake position faired over. The late MiG-15bis used a nosewheel that was similar to the MiG-17. Also the late MiG-15bis had a single piece gun blast panel in place of the two piece panel of the MiG-15 Fagot A.

When the MiG-15bis was first observed by the West, NATO gave the aircraft the reporting name Fagot B. Like the earlier MiG-15 Fagot A, the MiG-15bis was known in Soviet service as the *Samoljot Soldat* (aircraft of the soldier), while in Hungary the MiG-15bis was generally known as *Sas* or Eagle.

During the Cold War period, the MiG-15 saw action in various border incidents. Any Western aircraft that strayed beyond the *Iron Curtain* was attacked by MiG-15s. One of the first incidents involved a French DC-4 which was attacked in the Berlin Corridor on 29 April 1952. On 11 May 1952, a U.S. Navy PBM was intercepted over the Sea of Japan by two MiG-15s which conducted a total of six firing passes, but only inflicted minor damage to the PBM.

On 4 June 1952, a U.S. aircraft carrying U.S. High Commissioner Donnelly was buzzed by two Soviet MiG-15s over Austria. On 15 July 1952, a USAF RB-26 weather reconnaissance aircraft was attacked over the Yellow Sea by MiG-15s, and on 31 July 1952, a Navy PBM-5 was attacked in the same area by Soviet MiG-15s. Soviet MiG-15bis Fagot Bs buzzed and fired on a USAF C-47 in the Berlin corridor on 8 October 1952. Three Navy F9F Panthers were attacked by four MiG-15s over the Sea of Japan on 18 November 1952. This engagement saw two MiG-15s shot down and another damaged. One of the Panthers was damaged.

On 15 March 1953, an RB-50 exchanged fire with Soviet MiG-15s over the Pacific, east of Kamchatka. MiG-15s shot down a USAF RB-50 over the Sea of Japan on 29 July 1953. Another reconnaissance aircraft, escorted by sixteen fighters, was attacked by eight MiG-15s over the Yellow Sea on 22 January 1954. During the fighting one MiG-15 was shot down without loss to the American side. On 7 November 1954, a USAF RB-29 was shot down north of Hokkaido, Japan by MiG-15s. A USAF F-86 Sabre shot down a North Korean MiG-15 over the Sea of Japan on 5 February 1955. A Navy P2V-5 Neptune patrol bomber crash landed on Saint Lawrence Island after being attacked by Soviet MiG-15s over the Bering Sea on 22 June 1955.

This early production MiG-15bis, Red 55, was used for testing at the NII-VVS. Early production Fagot Bs retained the NS-23 cannons, identified by the long cannon fairings. The aircraft is also equipped with two 105 gallon (400 liter) drop tanks.

A MiG-15bis *Sas* (Eagle) of the Hungarian Air Force. The first MiG-15bis fighters were received by the Hungarian Air Force during early 1953 and received the nickname *Sas*. The Red tactical number has a thin White outline. The small antenna under the wingtip is the radio altimeter antenna.

SD-UPB

The SD-UPB (*Uvieliichennije podvyesnije baki*, increased belly tank) was a standard MiG-15bis (Red 850) fitted with two 79 gallon (300 liter) slipper tanks for a series of evaluation trials. This configuration later became standard on all production MiG-15bis fighters. This same aircraft was later converted to the MiG-17 prototype, with a different engine and wings.

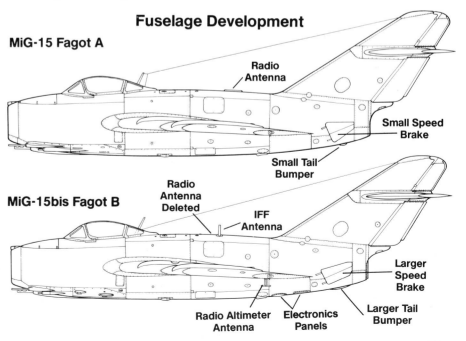

Fuselage Development

MiG-15 Fagot A

Radio Antenna

Small Speed Brake

Small Tail Bumper

MiG-15bis Fagot B

Radio Antenna Deleted

IFF Antenna

Radio Altimeter Antenna

Electronics Panels

Larger Speed Brake

Larger Tail Bumper

17

MiG-15bisS

The MiG-15bisS was a long range escort fighter with two 158.5 gallon (600 liter) drop tanks. It had a ceiling of 43,963 feet (13,400 meters) and a range of 1,566 miles (2,520 km). The 600 liter tank was also issued as standard equipment on production MiG-15bis and the S designation was dropped.

MiG-15bisF

The MiG-15bisF was a reconnaissance variant fitted with a pod under the nose containing either an AFA-1M or an AFP-21KT camera. The gun armament was deleted to save space and weight. There were only a small number built and all were used by the Soviet Air Force. The MiG-15bisF was popular and had the nickname *Fotobis*.

MiG-15bisR

The MiG-15bisR (R for *Rasvedtchik*, reconnaissance) was another reconnaissance variant of the Fagot B. Instead of carrying a pod with cameras, the camera installation, consisting of an AFA-1M camera and an AFP-21KT camera replaced the inboard NR-23 and the N-37 cannon, with the outboard NR-23 cannon being remained. Externally, the MiG-15bisR could be identified by the missing cannon fairings.

The cameras and some of their supporting equipment were placed under the main fuel tank which was reduced in size. To ensure sufficient range, the MiG-15bisR usually carried 600 liter underwing tanks. With the NFP-02 night illumination flare dispenser, it was possible to conduct night reconnaissance.

MiG-15ISh

The MiG-15ISh (*Istrebityel-Shturmovik*, Fighter-Assault aircraft) was an unsuccessful attempt to modify the MiG-15 for the close air support role that was being filled by the propeller driven Il-10M.

The MiG-15ISh was evaluated against the Il-40, a two seat attack aircraft powered by two Mikulin AM-5F jet engines. The Il-40 had demanding flying characteristics but was more heavily armed than the MiG-15ISh. Since the MiG-15bis was in full production and the Soviets did not want to put yet another aircraft type into series production, the established MiG-15bis was selected for modification and production.

Essentially, the MiG-15ISh was a standard production Fagot B with large underwing pylons which faired into the outboard wing fences. Each pylon could carry three bomb racks while internal gun armament remained the same as the standard MiG-15bis.

The MIG-15ISh could carry a number of different weapons on underwing pylons including FAB 50 bombs, FAB 100 general purpose bombs, ARS-212 and TRS-190 unguided missiles and ORO-57K rocket pods (eight S-5 57MM rockets).

Flight and armament trials with the MiG-15ISh revealed that the aircraft did not meet Air Force expectations and the project was cancelled.

Ground crews perform routine maintenance on the guns of a Hungarian Air Force MiG-15bis (Serial 31530802). The aircraft is jacked up on its nose and the cannon platform has been lowered. This simple system allowed for quick and easy access to the cannons, for both servicing and reloading.

A flight of Hungarian Air Force MiG-15bis *Sas* prepare to taxi out for a mission. The three digit tactical numbers are Red with a thin White outline. The landing light, carried in the intake splitter on the MiG-15, was relocated to the port wing on the MiG-15bis and the nose position faired over.

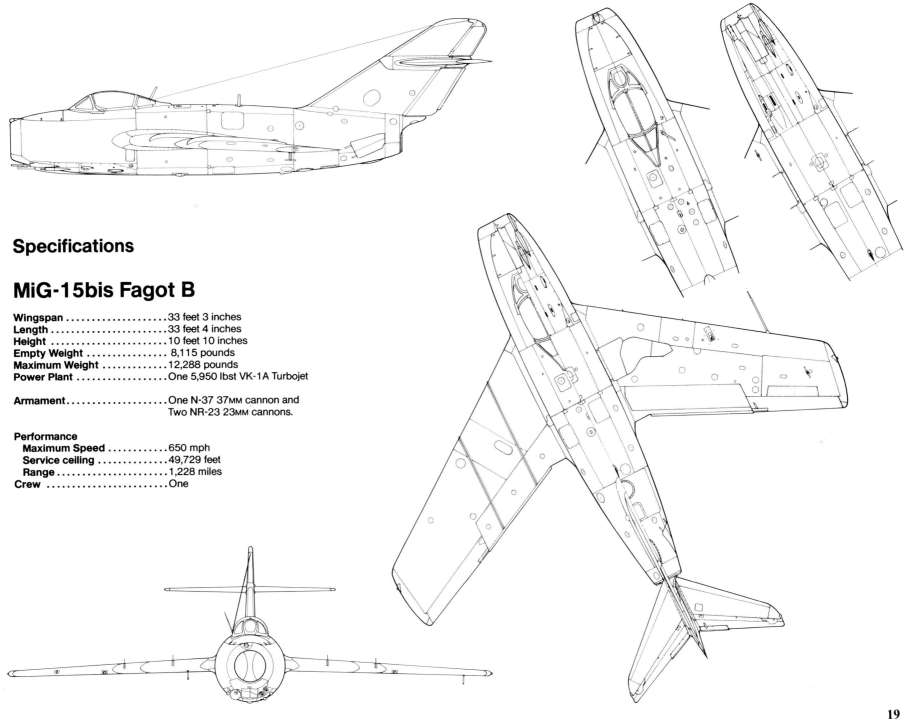

Specifications

MiG-15bis Fagot B

Wingspan .33 feet 3 inches
Length .33 feet 4 inches
Height . . . . .10 feet 10 inches
Empty Weight . . . . 8,115 pounds
Maximum Weight . . . . .12,288 pounds
Power Plant . . . . .One 5,950 lbst VK-1A Turbojet

Armament .One N-37 37ᴍᴍ cannon and
Two NR-23 23ᴍᴍ cannons.

Performance
  Maximum Speed . . . . .650 mph
  Service ceiling . . . . .49,729 feet
  Range . . . . .1,228 miles
Crew . . . . .One

This MiG-15bis, Red 23, was used for flight tests at Ramenskoye. The tactical number was Red with a thin Black outline. The fin tip and SRU-O IFF antenna were Black.

Hungarian Air Force pilots are given instructions in front of their MiG-15bis fighters before a mission. All the aircraft carry the squadron's triangle marking on the fin. The center MiG-15 has a Red arrow marking on the slipper tank. These squadron markings were first introduced during 1954, only used by ground-attack units.

MiG-15bis Aerial Refueling

The Soviet Air Force conducted various trials aimed at increasing the range of the MiG-15bis. Beside using standard underwing fuel tanks, some rather unorthodox methods were tested.

One of the first ideas which was tried was that of towing escort fighters by bombers in which a pair of MiG-15bis would be towed by a Tu-4 Bull (the Soviet copy of the Boeing B-29). The towing system was developed by the Experimental Design Bureau of Alexander Yakovlev, the designer of the Yak-3 and Yak-9 fighters. The towing system was called *GARPUN* by the Yakovelev OKB.

The trials were successful, but revealed one unacceptable shortcoming. With the engine shut down the cockpit could not be heated. As a result, pilots would suffer the effects of the cold even during short duration flights. With no way of providing alternative cockpit heating, the project was cancelled.

Another experiment to increase the range of the MiG-15bis was by aerial refueling. The tanker aircraft for these experiments was a modified Tu-4 Bull and between 1952 and 1955 at least twelve Tu-4s were converted into the tanker role. There were various configurations used, but in the case of the MiG-15bis project, two booms were installed on the wings to supply fuel to the fighters and two MiG-15bis Fagot Bs could be refueled at the same time.

The MiG-15bis fighters converted for the evaluation had a refueling probe mounted on the port side of the nose. Apart from the fixed probe and internal piping, the aircraft were standard MiG-15bis fighters.

The successful trials were the first aerial refuelings of fighter aircraft in the history of Soviet Military Aviation. There were a small batch of MiG-15bis aircraft built with the fixed refueling probe and these saw limited operational service, but carried no special designation.

Armament

MiG-15bis
(Early)

MiG-15bis
(Late)

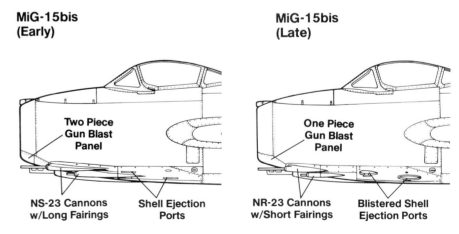

Two Piece Gun Blast Panel

One Piece Gun Blast Panel

NS-23 Cannons w/Long Fairings   Shell Ejection Ports

NR-23 Cannons w/Short Fairings   Blistered Shell Ejection Ports

A group of Hungarian Air Force pilots are given a briefing on the cockpit layout of the MiG-15bis . The small round rod in front of the cockpit on the port side of the nose is the nose-wheel down indicator rod.

A MiG-15bis of the Cuban *Fuerza Aerea Revolucionaria*. A small number of MiG-15bis aircraft were in Cuba during the Bay of Pigs invasion; however, there were only ten qualified pilots on the island. The rest were in the Soviet Union undergoing conversion training.

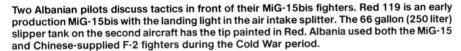

Two Albanian pilots discuss tactics in front of their MiG-15bis fighters. Red 119 is an early production MiG-15bis with the landing light in the air intake splitter. The 66 gallon (250 liter) slipper tank on the second aircraft has the tip painted in Red. Albania used both the MiG-15 and Chinese-supplied F-2 fighters during the Cold War period.

A new production MiG-15bis, Red 3, of the East German Air Force during the Fall of 1956. The German Democratic Republic was the last WARSAW Pact member to be equipped with the MiG-15bis. This aircraft carries the early style national markings used between 1956 and late 1959. The single digit tactical number was used for a brief period before it was changed to a two digit system.

The ground crew of an East German MiG-15bis, Red 48, reports to the pilot that the aircraft is ready for flight. These crewmen had been part of the *Volkspolizei Luft* (Air Police), which formed the personnel cadre for the East German Air Force.

A MiG-15bis of the Algerian Air Force. The Algerian Air Force was established during 1962 with Soviet instructors and aircraft. The MiG-15bis was first employed as an interceptor. Late in their operational service lives, some twenty surviving aircraft were transferred to the fighter-bomber role.

East German ground crewmen perform routine maintenance on this MiG-15bis, Red 9. The Black uniforms of the ground crew were a carryover from the Luftwaffe of World War II. The two Black boxes at the rear of the open equipment bay are the transmitter and receiver for the R-800 radio set.

This MiG-15bis of the Hungarian Air Force was damaged when it overshot the runway on landing and crashed into a Soviet built ZIS truck. The impact knocked the fairings off the two NR-23 cannons.

A Hungarian Air Force pilot poses in front of his MiG-15bis, Red 681. The aircraft was a late production MiG-15bis with a MiG-17 type nose wheel. The Hungarians named their aircraft after animals and birds, a tradition carried over from World War II, The Fagot A was the *Jaguar*, while the MiG-15bis was the *Sas* (Eagle).

Ground crews work on Red 2404, an early production MiG-15bis of the Romanian Air Force at Deveselu Airfield during 1962. This aircraft carries the RV-2 radio altimeter antenna mounted above the NS-37 cannon fairing. The antenna was later relocated to the wing root.

Toward the end of their operational service lives, the Hungarian Air Force used the MiG-15bis *Sas* in the ground support role and camouflaged the aircraft with the national insignia being carried on both the upper and lower surfaces of the wings.

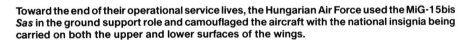

This MiG-15bis, Red 346, of the Polish Air Force was the first intact MiG-15 Fagot inspected by Western intelligence. On 5 March 1953, LT Franciszek Garecki of the 28th Fighter Regiment based at Slupsk on the Baltic coast, defected during a routine patrol. He landed on Bornholm Island (Danish territory). The aircraft was returned on 22 March 1953, aboard a Polish merchant ship.

The MiG-15bis found at Bradavil by the Israeli Navy was delivered by vessel to Hatzor AFB where it was to be repaired and flown again. After it arrived, it was discovered that the damage was more extensive than first thought and the aircraft was used as a war memorial. (Shlomo Kleszcelski-Aloni).

CAPT Yak Nevo, vice commander of 101 Squadron, IDF/AF, damaged this MiG-15bis of the Egyptian Air Force over the Sinai on 31 October 1956. Fortunately, the Egyptian pilot made a forced landing at Bradavil, where it was later discovered by the Israeli Navy. The MiG-15bis carries early style Egyptian markings with Green identification stripes on wing tips and fuselage. (Shlomo Kleszcelski-Aloni)

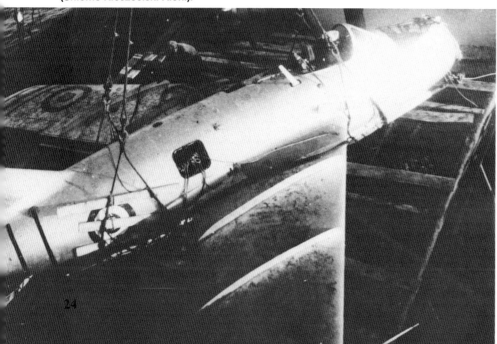

24

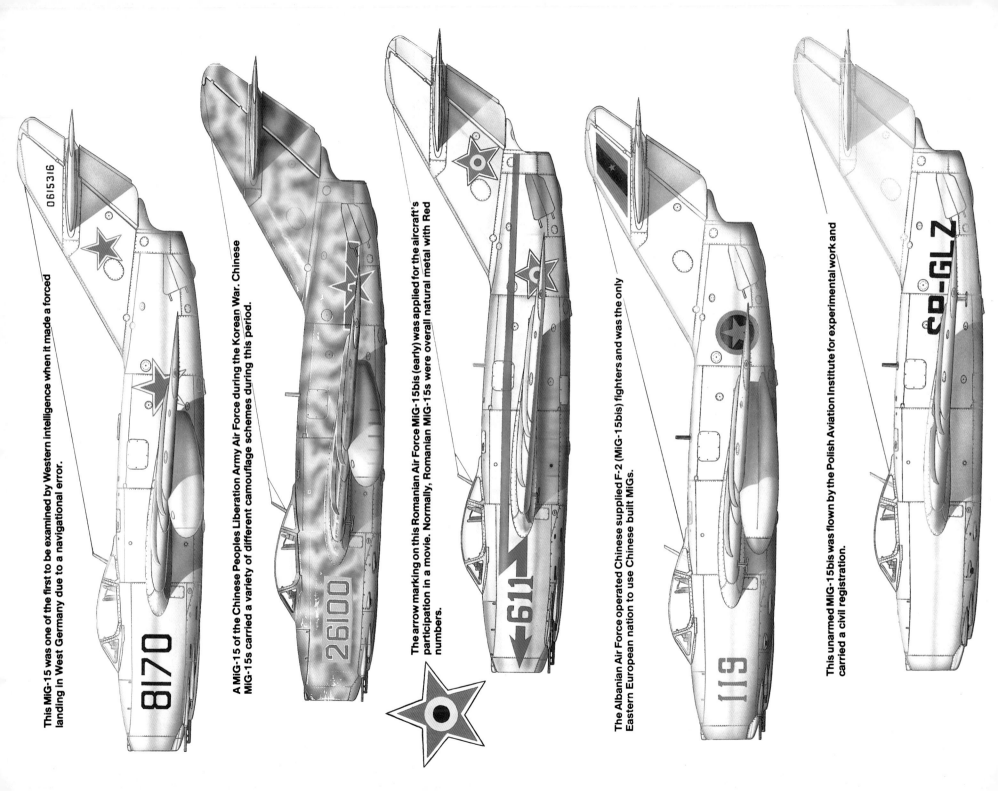

This MiG-15 was one of the first to be examined by Western intelligence when it made a forced landing in West Germany due to a navigational error.

A MiG-15 of the Chinese Peoples Liberation Army Air Force during the Korean War. Chinese MiG-15s carried a variety of different camouflage schemes during this period.

The arrow marking on this Romanian Air Force MiG-15bis (early) was applied for the aircraft's participation in a movie. Normally, Romanian MiG-15s were overall natural metal with Red numbers.

The Albanian Air Force operated Chinese supplied F-2 (MiG-15bis) fighters and was the only Eastern European nation to use Chinese built MiGs.

This unarmed MiG-15bis was flown by the Polish Aviation Institute for experimental work and carried a civil registration.

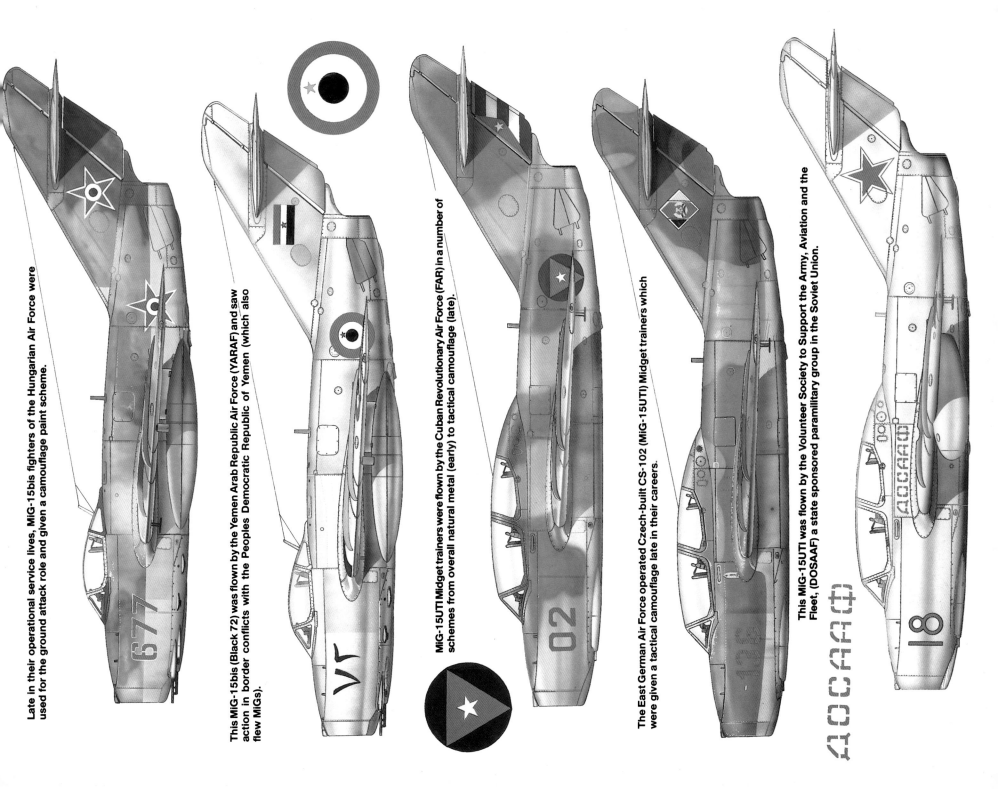

Late in their operational service lives, MiG-15bis fighters of the Hungarian Air Force were used for the ground attack role and given a camouflage paint scheme.

This MiG-15bis (Black 72) was flown by the Yemen Arab Republic Air Force (YARAF) and saw action in border conflicts with the Peoples Democratic Republic of Yemen (which also flew MiGs).

MiG-15UTI Midget trainers were flown by the Cuban Revolutionary Air Force (FAR) in a number of schemes from overall natural metal (early) to tactical camouflage (late).

The East German Air Force operated Czech-built CS-102 (MiG-15UTI) Midget trainers which were given a tactical camouflage late in their careers.

This MiG-15UTI was flown by the Volunteer Society to Support the Army, Aviation and the Fleet, (DOSAAF) a state sponsored paramilitary group in the Soviet Union.

A line up of East German Air Force MiG-15bis fighters with the late style national markings introduced during late 1959. The insignia was carried on the fin and on both the upper and lower wing surfaces. This insignia did not change again until the German Democratic Republic disbanded on 3 October 1990.

This Soviet built MiG-15bis (Serial 1370086) was transferred to the Polish Aviation Institute on 18 November 1958 and given the civil registration SP-GLZ. The fin was painted Yellow and the registration was in Black. The MiG-15bis was used in research work to launch sounding rockets, like this SPD-6 rocket, from a special wing pylon.

This MiG-15bis, Red 2404, of the Romanian Air Force carries the roundel style national insignia introduced during 1985. MiG-15bis aircraft are allocated to MiG-21 fighter and IAR-93 ground attack regiments for use as weather reconnaissance aircraft and are based at Craiova, Gearmata and Focsani.

This MiG-15bis, Red 2057, of the North Korean Peoples Air Force was flown to South Korea by its pilot, Ro Kim Suk on 21 September 1953. Shortly after it landed at Kimpo Air Base near Seoul, the aircraft was parked in a secured hangar.

The armament platform of the MiG-15bis is examined by USAF armament specialists. The simple, but effective way of maintaining the cannons surprised the Americans. The entire gun platform was lowered by the cables on the front and rear of the platform. Maintenance and re-arming of the F-86 was much more difficult.

The USAF evaluated the MiG-15bis (Serial 2015337) at Kadena Air Base on Okinawa. The pitot tube on the port side of the fuselage in front of the cockpit was added by the USAF for the trials. The side number, 616, was selected by CAPT Tom Collins, who had flown F-86s with this same number.

The MiG-15bis was also tested at Wright-Patterson Air Force Base, Ohio. After initial testing at Kadena the aircraft was disassembled and shipped to Wright-Patterson where the components were closely examined. During 1954, the aircraft was re-assembled for flight testing at Wright-Patterson and Eglin AFB.

The SD-UPB was basically an early MiG-15bis with 300 liter slipper tanks, instead of the previously used 250 liter slipper tanks. No SPU-O IFF aerial is carried on the fuselage. "Black 850" has a Red silhouette on the nose. The same aircraft was later converted into the first MiG-17F prototype, receiving new wings and engine.

The MiG-15bisR prototype on the ramp at Ramenskoye carried no national markings or tactical number. The prototype carried a single NR-23 cannon with the camera ports housed in the large fairing behind the gun.

The MiG-15ISh prototype on display armed with two FAB 100 (220 pound) bombs on the enlarged weapons pylon. The pylon was able to accommodate three FAB 100 bombs, or a variety of other weapons. The project proved unsuccessful and the aircraft was cancelled.

A MiG-15ISh could be easily distinguished from a standard MiG-15 by the enlarged weapons pylon faired into the outboard wing fence. The rocket pod is an ORO-57K eight shot pod.

This MiG-15bis R served as a test aircraft with the NII-VVS. It carries a single NR-23 cannon on port side of the fuselage and lacks the standard SRU-O IFF aerial on the fuselage. The camera was installed in the position normally occupied by the second NR-23 cannon. The aircraft carries a small aircraft silhouette marking on the nose.

The Lim-2R was a Polish built variant of the MiG-15bisF photographic reconnaissance aircraft with the AFA camera pod on the port nose underside. The aircraft carries 79 gallon (300 liter) slipper tanks.

This MiG-15bis, Red 342, is refueled from a Tu-4 tanker conversion. The three digit tactical number was unusual and was only used on experimental and training units. There were a number of MiG-15bis aircraft equipped with the aerial refueling probe, but these received no special designation.

A pair of MiG-15bis are refueled by a Tupolev Tu-4 Bull tanker conversion. There were at least twelve Tu-4 bombers converted to the tanker role during 1952. The MiG-15bis trials were the first successful aerial refueling of jet aircraft in the USSR.

Foreign Built MiG-15s

Czech S-102/103

The *Letectvo CSLA* (Czech Air Force) flew both Soviet built and Czech manufactured variants of the MiG-15. Based on a long Czech tradition, the first letter of the aircraft designation denotes the role of an aircraft with fighters receiving the letter "S" (for *Stihac*, fighter). The letter is followed by a sequential number. This system was used on both domestic and imported aircraft. When the Czechs received their first MiG-15s they became the S-102 in the Czech inventory. During the late 1950s, this system was dropped in favor of the original Soviet designation.

License production of the MiG-15 began during 1951 at the Rudeho Letova factory at Prague. During 1953, the entire production line was moved to the newly established Aero Vodochody plant on the outskirts of Prague. Production of the S-102 Fagot A ended in 1954 in favor of the more advanced S-103 (MiG-15bis).

In addition to the airframe, the Czech Motorlet factory was licensed to manufacture the RD-45 under the designation M-05. The first Czech manufactured power plants were delivered during 1952. Motorlet later produced the VK-1 power plant for the MiG-15bis under the designation M-06 and a total of some 5,000 engines were produced in Czechoslovakia.

During 1950, a cadre of pilots were trained in the Soviet Union and a number of Soviet instructors under the command of CAPT Sakurov were posted to the Czech Air Force to conduct conversion training the following year. Many of these early MiG-15 pilots later became instructors for other Czech pilots. By 1953, a large number of Czech fighter units had been re-equipped with the MiG-15.

The Czechs also developed two special variants of the MiG-15:

MiG-15T

The MiG-15T (*Tahac*, Tug) was a target tow variant for anti-aircraft gun units. The target winch was operated by an L-03 generator, which allowed the target to be towed behind the aircraft at a safe distance, then reeled in after the mission.

MiG-15SB

The MiG-15SB (*Stihac Bombardovaci*, fighter-bomber) was a Czech developed fighter-bomber variant of the MiG-15, which saw considerable use in the Czech Air Force. The MiG-15SB was fitted with two weapons pylons, one inboard and one outboard of the standard slipper tank. These pylons could accommodate a wide range of armament, such as LR-130 rockets, SR-55 rocket pods, RBK-250 260 pound bombs or OFAB-100M high explosive incendiary bombs. With the underwing fuel tanks removed, a total of six bomb racks were available for short range missions. The MiG-15SB was equipped with two gun sights, a PBP-1B optical gun sight in addition to the standard ASP-3N gyro gun sight. The MiG-15SB also had provision for two RATO-rockets which were mounted on the rear fuselage to shorten the takeoff run with a full bomb load.

To meet a request from the North Vietnamese government, the Czechs converted an MiG-15SB to accommodate the two K-13 (AA-2) Atoll air-to-air missiles. To mount the fire control system for the missiles, the starboard NS-37 cannon was deleted and an infrared sensor was mounted in the cannon fairing. The two K-13 missiles were carried on rails mounted on the inboard wing pylons beside the wing tanks. Tests with the conversion proved to be disappointing and the project was cancelled. Only one MiG-15SB missile carrier conversion was completed.

These Czech manufactured S-103 Fagot Bs all have the fin tip painted in Blue. Czechoslovakia was the sole WARSAW Pact nation that painted the tactical number (in the case of the MiG-15, four digit numbers in Black) on the rear of the fuselage. All other member nations painted the tactical number on the nose.

Initially, the S-103 carried a two letter/two digit tactical code on the nose in Black. This system was later changed in favor of a four digit tactical number painted on the rear of the fuselage. The tactical numbers of MiG-15s and S-103s were always in Black.

A Czech Air Force pilot poses in front of his S-103 Fagot B, Black LN-03. The S-103 was the Czech-built equivalent of the MiG-15bis, built by Aero Vodochody on the outskirts of Prague. The pilot's flight suit was standard for WARSAW Pact forces during the fifties and early sixties.

A Czech built S-103, Black 3234, taxis past two Polish Lim-2 fighters during the 2nd Culture and Sports Meeting held at Cottbus, East Germany between 30 August and 1 September 1957. During the air show, Czech, Polish, Soviet and East German military aircraft participated. Black 3234 carries a Red arrow marking that extends over the wing upper surfaces.

A Czech-built S-103 Fagot B of the Czech Air force aerobatic team trails smoke from the wing mounted smoke generators during an air show. The nose band is Red and the Arrow marking is Red with a White outline.

These Czech built S-103 (MiG-15bis) Fagot Bs carry the later style tactical numbers in Black behind the wing. The small T antenna under the wing is the radio altimeter antenna.

Pylon Development

MiG-15bis/S-103

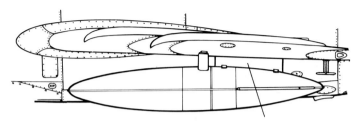

Single Pylon For Bombs/Fuel Tanks

MiG-15SB

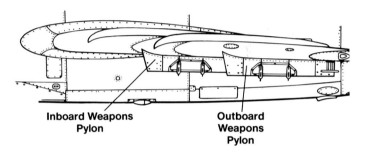

Inboard Weapons Pylon

Outboard Weapons Pylon

Atoll Missile Pylon

MiG-15SB Missile Carrier

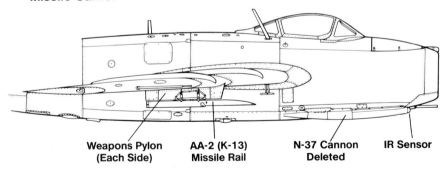

Weapons Pylon (Each Side)

AA-2 (K-13) Missile Rail

N-37 Cannon Deleted

IR Sensor

AA-2 (K-13) Atoll AAM

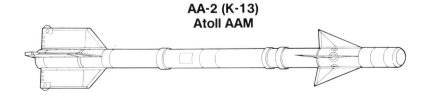

Czech Air Force MiG-15SBs on the ramp at Mosnov-Ostrava airfield. The MiG-15SB was a Czech built fighter bomber variant of the MiG-15bis. The aircraft had an additional weapons pylon installed inboard and outboard of the standard bomb rack. These MiG-15SBs carry the crest of the city of Ostrava on the nose. Applying the crest of the city where a unit was based was popular until the mid-sixties when the government halted the use of insignia and crests for security reasons.

Polish Lim-1/2

The first Soviet manufactured MiG-15 for the Polish Air Force arrived in crates during June of 1951, at the home base of the *1 Pulk Lotnictwa Mysliwskiego "Warszawa"* (1st Fighter Wing) outside Minsk-Mazowiecki. Even before these first aircraft had arrived in Poland, the technology transfer from the USSR to the *Panstwowe Zaklady Lotnicze (PZL)* factory at Mielec had begun in preparation for the manufacture of the MiG-15 in Poland. During May of 1951, PZL received construction documentation and a MiG-15 to serve as a pattern aircraft (serial 113074).

Imported Soviet built MiG-15 Fagot As were simply called MiG-15s in Polish service, while the license built aircraft were named Lim-1 (Lim for *Licencyjny mysliwiec*, License fighter). The first MiG-15s assembled at the PZL factory at Mielec were assembled from components supplied by the Soviet Union. The first of these aircraft flew for the first time on 22 July 1951, with Eugeniusz Pniewski at the controls. The Lim-1 had the factory designation "1A" and the first example assembled was 1A-01-001, the first two digits denoted the batch-number and the last three digits the number of the aircraft within the block.

During 1952, six Lim-1s were produced, all assembled from parts delivered from the Soviet Union. Series production started in January of 1953, and while the airframe was produced at Mielec, the RD-45F power plants were built at the WSK plant in Rzeszow under the designation Lis-1 (*Licencyjny silnik*, License engine).

There were twelve production batches of Lim-1s produced for a total of 227 aircraft. The last Lim-1 rolled out from the Mielec factory on 1 September 1954. A number of Lim-1s were converted to the target tug configuration with the lower NS-23 cannon deleted and target towing equipment fitted in its place under the nose.

Lim-1.5

The Lim-1.5, called *Lim-pol tora* (Lim-one and a half) was a Lim-1 with the Lis-1 (RD-45F) power plant and the small speed brakes standard of the Fagot A, but with a number of avionics upgrades from the later MiG-15bis. The aircraft carried a more powerful R-800 radio, an ARK-5 radio compass, an RV-2 radio altimeter and an SRU-0 IFF system.

There were no new Lim-1.5 produced, all aircraft being conversions from standard Lim-1s. The aircraft were converted and modernized at the LZR (*Lotniczych Zakladach Remontowych*, Aviation Repair Factory). The designation Lim-1.5 was unofficial and did not affect the aircraft's serial number.

Lim-2

In addition to the Lim-1 (MiG-15) Poland also produced the MiG-15bis under license as the Lim-2. Production of the Lim-2 began during 1954, and these aircraft were identical to late production Soviet MiG-15bis aircraft.

The Lim-2R was the Polish built version of the MiG-15bisF reconnaissance aircraft with the camera pod mounted on the port side of the lower fuselage behind the nose wheel well in place of the rear NR-23 gun.

With the end of the Cold War, a number of Lim-1 and LiM-2 aircraft have been sold on the western market to private collectors, especially in the United States and England.

A Polish built Lim-1.5 taxies in after a mission. The Lim-1.5 was a Lim-1 (MiG-15) with Lim-2 (MiG-15bis) avionics. These converted aircraft were upgraded with RV-2 radio altimeter antennas and a SPU-0 IFF antenna. They retained the RD-45F power plant and small speed brakes. Red 21 has the fin tip and lower part of the rudder in Red.

A Polish-built Lim-1, Red 004, is hooked to an American-built Lend Lease Dodge weapons carrier for towing to a new parking position. These vehicles were delivered to the USSR as Lend Lease aid and after the war a number were passed to countries within Moscow's sphere of influence.

A Lim-2 is hidden under camouflage netting during a field exercise. During the exercise, the aircraft were flown from highways. Red 607 was one of the first production Lim-2s powered by a Polish produced version of the VK-1A power plant built during early 1955. The engine was produced by W.S.K. at Rzeszow under the designation Lis-2.

This Lim-1 (Serial 1A-11-010) is equipped with target towing equipment behind the nose-wheel bay. The Soviet designation for such a conversion was the MiG-15T. This variant was used to tow a large banner behind the aircraft on a wire.

Target Tow

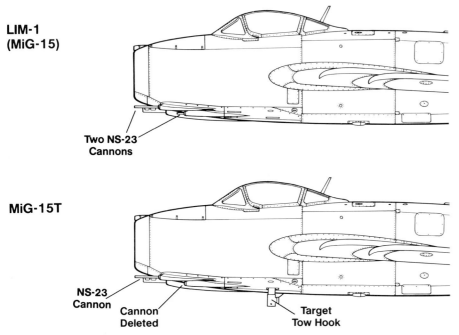

LIM-1 (MiG-15)

Two NS-23 Cannons

MiG-15T

NS-23 Cannon

Cannon Deleted

Target Tow Hook

Ground crews refuel a Polish built Lim-1 (Serial 1A-11-010). This aircraft has been converted to a target tug, with the target towing equipment under the fuselage. The lower NS-23 cannon has been deleted and the tow hook was located in the cannon shell ejection port.

Ground crews work on a Polish Lim-2 fighter. The wing root walkway has been covered with canvas to protect the wing from damage by the mechanics. Between the wing fences are two Black and White indicator rods. The rear most rod is the flaps down indicator and the forward rod is the landing gear down indicator.

Refueling crews refuel a line of Lim-2s (foreground) and Lim-1s (background). The fuel trucks are Soviet built ZIS-150 tank trucks. The aircraft carries 105 gallon (400 liter) drop tanks. The small opening on the fuselage is the signal flare launcher port.

A lineup of Polish Lim-2s on a Polish airfield during the late 1950s. Almost every aircraft carries a different style of tactical number. The rudder on most of the aircraft is in Red denoting that it was assigned to the first Squadron within the Regiment.

This Polish fighter regiment is equipped with Lim-2s. The aircraft in the foreground has the nose of the 105 gallon (400 liter) drop tank painted in Red bordered with a thin Black stripe. Polish aircraft do not carry the national insignia on the upper wing surfaces.

A regiment of Lim-2s stand by for the signal to begin their formation takeoff as part of a flyby for a national celebration during the 1950s. A number of the aircraft have the nose of the drop tank in Red, bordered in Black.

A Polish radio technician services the radios of this Lim-2. The gun barrels and air intake are covered to protect them from the weather. When no ammunition was carried, a balance weight was placed in the equipment bay in front of the cockpit.

Armament crews service the cannons of a Lim-2 (Serial 1B-01-020). The fairings of both the N-37 and NR-23 cannons have been removed in preparation of lowering the cannon platform. The ground crewman in the middle has the handle that controls the built-in winch used to lower and raise the platform.

A Polish Air Force pilot deplanes from a new production Lim-2 (Serial 1B-01-006). This aircraft was the sixth Lim-2 built by the W.S.K. Factory at Mielec and was delivered during May of 1954. The aircraft was powered by a Soviet supplied VK-1A power plant. Lim stands for *Licencyjny Mysliwiec* or License Fighter.

Two Polish Lim-2s prepare to depart on a routine patrol mission. The rear aircraft, Red 314, (Serial 1B-03-014) has a Red rudder and a Red band on the upper half of the rear fuselage. The starting cart is an East German unit, built by *VEB Flugzeugwerke* in Dresden, East Germany.

A Polish Lim-2R (Serial 1B-10-004) reconnaissance aircraft. The Lim-2R carried an AFA camera pod on the port side of the lower fuselage in place of one of the NR-23 cannons. These aircraft were used in the tactical reconnaissance role.

A pair of Polish Air Force Lim-2s conduct a combat patrol near the Polish border. The aircraft in the background, Red 1120, (Serial 1B-01-120) is now on permanent exhibit at the Royal Air Force Museum at Hendon, England. The aircraft arrived in England during 1986.

Chinese Variants

MiG-15/J-2

During March of 1950, China's newly-established Ministry of Heavy Industry formed a team under Vice Minister Liu Ding to establish a modern national aircraft industry in as little time as possible. Since they would be starting from the ground up it was an extraordinarily ambitious project for a technologically backward country.

The main source for new aircraft technology and manufacturing know-how was the Soviet Union. In October of 1951, an agreement was reached under which some 847 Soviet experts and advisers arrived in China to instruct the Chinese on the license production of the MiG-15bis fighter. Preparations were made at the Shenyang Aircraft Factory for production of both the aircraft and the VK-1A engine, with a goal of producing the first aircraft by the end of 1957. By the time the production line was established, it had become clear that the facility would be better put to use producing the MiG-15's successor, the MiG-17 Fresco and the project was cancelled. As a result, no MiG-15bis fighters were ever built in China.

While MiG-15s were not built in China, the aircraft (known as the J-2 in Chinese service) was imported in large numbers and the Shenyang facility did conduct overhauls and modifications of these aircraft. The VK-1A engine was manufactured in China under the designation WP-5A and used to power the Chinese built variant of the Il-28 bomber, the H-5.

Considerable experience with modern aircraft design was gained by the overhaul and repair of damaged MiG-15s. During the Korean war, the Shenyang facility repaired some 534 MiG-15 and MiG-15bis aircraft between 1951 and 1953. One modification that appeared on MiG-15bis aircraft in China was the addition of an access panel on the port side of the nose. This panel was common to the MiG-17F and was added to the MiG-15s during periodic overhaul.

As the MiG-15 was superseded in Chinese service by the MiG-17F (J-5) large numbers of MiG-15s became available for export. These aircraft were exported under the Chinese export designations F-2 (MiG-15bis) and FT-2 (MiG-15UTI) to Albania, Bangladesh, North Korea, Pakistan, Sudan, Tanzania and North Vietnam.

A flight of MiG-15bis fighters of the Chinese Peoples Liberation Army Air Force patrol over China. The aircraft in the foreground has no national insignia on the wing uppersurfaces, while the next aircraft has the insignia visible on the starboard wing. The last aircraft in the flight has a Black slipper tank.

Chinese pilots are briefed for their next mission in front of their MiG-15bis fighters. Known as the J-2 in Chinese service, the MiG-15 was not actually built in China, but the Chinese did carry out rebuilds and modification programs on their Soviet-supplied MiG-15bis aircraft.

Ground crews prepare a Chinese Liberation Army Air Force MiG-15 for a mission during the Korean war. The Fagot Bs carry an unusual camouflage of mottled Dark Green, Light Green and Sand uppersurfaces over Light Blue undersurfaces. The Red tactical number, 26100, has a White outline.

Access Panel

MiG-15bis aircraft of a Chinese fighter regiment on the flight line of the State Aircraft Factory at Shenyang in Manchuria. These aircraft were reassembled from Soviet-supplied components, not built in China. The aircraft have sequential tactical numbers.

MiG-15bis

**MiG-15bis
(Chinese Modified)**

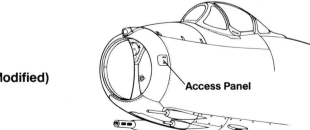

Access Panel

MiG-15UTI Midget

During 1949, a year after the MiG-15 was introduced into series production, work began on an advanced combat trainer variant of the basic MiG-15. The project was given the MiG-OKB project code ST and the Soviet military designation I-312T.

The first prototype flew for the first time during 1949, and was followed by two others. These aircraft were basically two-seat conversions of the MiG-15. The first prototype had the radio antenna fairing behind the canopy on the fuselage spine, but this was deleted on the second prototype. The ST prototypes passed their State Acceptance trials quickly and the first production UTMiG-15 left the assembly line of State Aircraft Factory Number One at Frunze airfield during late 1949 (there have been a number of designations for the MiG-15 trainer, such as UTMiG-15, UMiG-15 and UTIMiG-15. These were all used in various operational and maintenance manuals until finally the designation MiG-15UTI was assigned as standard.)

Compared with the single-seat MiG-15 Fagot, the MiG-15UTI differed primarily in the front fuselage. To make room for the second cockpit, the fuselage was stretched by 3.28 feet (1 meter) and the capacity of the main fuel tank was reduced from 330 gallons (1,250 liters) to 200 gallons (760 liters). To make up for this loss in internal fuel a small additional 20 gallon (78 liters) fuel tank was located under the front cockpit. The two cockpits were separated, each with their own individual pressure systems and a glass screen was installed between each cockpit. This was done to ensure no loss of cabin pressure should one cockpit canopy be lost.

The front cockpit controls are automatically disconnected whenever the instructor in the rear cockpit takes control. The only difference between the front and the rear cockpit layouts was that the rear cockpit lacked a gun sight. The rear canopy opens to the rear, while the front canopy opens to starboard. The communications system used in the MiG-15UTI is the SPU-2P intercom.

The first MiG-15UTIs were armed with a single UBK-E 12.7MM machine gun on the port side of the nose. This same gun had been used on various World War II aircraft such as the Pe-2 and Tu-2. It had a rate of fire of 1,000 rounds per minute and an ammunition capacity of 150 rounds. Later MiG-15UTIs were equipped with an A-12.7 machine gun, which had been developed during 1948 for use on the Tu-4 Bull. The weapon was subsequently used on various helicopters such as the Mi-4A, Mi-6T and the Mi-24A as well as the MiG-15UTI. A number of MiG-15UTIs were armed with a single NR-23 cannon. When carrying the cannon the gun blister on the fuselage was slightly larger and the internal ammunition capacity was reduced to 80 rounds.

The MiG-15UTI was progressively updated at the same time as the single seat MiG-15, although all Soviet and Czech built MiG-15UTIs retained the smaller Fagot A style speed brakes, even after being retrofitted with the VK-1 power plant of the MiG-15bis.

Early MiG-15UTIs lacked the SRU-O IFF blade antenna and the RV-2 radio altimeter antennas. The aircraft had a single gun blast panel on the port side of nose and the majority of the MiG-15UTIs did not have the notched wing fence of the MiG-15bis. Like the single seaters, the MiG-15UTI could carry drop tanks, both slipper style and the larger underwing style.

When NATO discovered the existence of the MiG-15UTI, they assigned it the reporting name Midget. The Soviets nicknamed the MiG-15UTI *Babushka* (Grandmother) and *Matushka* (good old woman).

The MiG-15UTI has had a long operational career and remains in service some forty years after its maiden flight. The aircraft is still in operational use in various air forces as

The first MiG-15UTI prototype carried the MIG-OKB project code ST-1 and the military designation I-312T. The aircraft was tested by the NII-VVS during 1949. The prototype retained the Fagot A radio antenna fairing on the fuselage spine and lacked RV-2 radio altimeter and SPU-O IFF antennas.

Fuselage Development

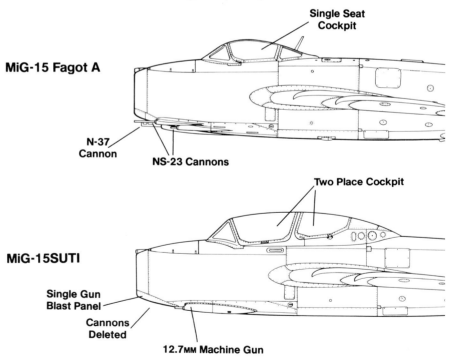

Single Seat Cockpit

MiG-15 Fagot A

N-37 Cannon

NS-23 Cannons

Two Place Cockpit

MiG-15SUTI

Single Gun Blast Panel

Cannons Deleted

12.7MM Machine Gun

a trainer and is also used for weather reconnaissance flights. Since there were no two-seat MiG-17 or MiG-19 trainers built, the Midget was also used as an advanced trainer leading to the Fresco and Farmer.

The MIG-15UTI has served in most of the countries using the single seat Fagot in addition to other countries which use Midget as a lead in trainer for the MiG-21. Midgets have been delivered to Afghanistan, Albania, Algeria, Angola, Bulgaria, China, Cuba, Czechoslovakia, Egypt, Finland, German Democratic Republic, Guinea, Hungary, Indonesia, Iraq, North Korea, Mali, Mongolia, Morocco, Nigeria, Poland, Romania, Somalia, South Yemen, North Yemen, Sri Lanka, Syria, Tanzania, Uganda and Vietnam.

Czech CS-102

During 1955, production of the MiG-15UTI was begun at the Aero Vodochody plant on the outskirts of Prague. In Czech service the type received the designation CS-102 (CS, *Cvicny Stihac* or training fighter). There were a substantial number of Czech-built CS-102s exported to other WARSAW Pact members as well as to Iraq and Indonesia. A number of CS-102s were fitted with an enlarged fairing over the UBK-E machine gun with a redesigned shell casing ejection port, which was V-shaped.

SBLim-1/SBLim-2

There were no MiG-15UTI trainers produced in Poland and a substantial part of the original Midget trainer fleet were imported from Czechoslovakia. The first Soviet-built MiG-15UTIs were delivered during 1951.

When the MiG-15 was superseded in Polish Air Force service, it was decided to convert a number of these aircraft to the UTI configuration. As a result the Polish Aviation Repair Factory begun to convert Lim-1 (MiG-15) aircraft into two-seat trainers under the designation SBSLim-1 (SB, *Szkolno-bojowy*, Training Combat).

Later, a number of these aircraft were modified with the engine and rear fuselage of the Lim-2 (MiG-15bis), these aircraft were designated SBLim-2 and featured enlarged speed brakes and an enlarged tail bumper.

During 1965, the Polish Air Force decided to use a number of SBLim-1 trainers in a fast FAC (forward air controller) type role. These aircraft operated in conjunction with ground troops, providing reconnaissance and acting as a forward observer for artillery fire.

The aircraft were converted at the Aviation Repair Factory at Bydgoszcz, with the rear controls being replaced by a navigation panel. The armament was increased to two NR-23 cannons, both being carried on the port side of the nose with 80 rounds of ammunition per gun. During 1968, the Polish Air Force began to convert a number of SBLim-2 aircraft to this standard. Initially these aircraft were designated the SBLim-1 Art and SBLilm-2 Art (Art for *Artyleryjski*, Artillery) but this was soon shortened to SBLim-1A and SBLim-2A. A few aircraft were equipped with a pod on starboard side on the rear fuselage housing an AFA-39 camera. A number of aircraft carried an AFA-BAF/21S camera mounted between the two ammunition boxes on the gun platform in the nose.

Later, a number of SBLim-2As were converted back into advanced two-seat trainers. The navigator compartment was deleted and a full set of dual controls were reinstalled in the rear cockpit. These aircraft were designated a SBLim-2Ms and they retained the twin NR-23 cannons on the port side of the nose. Both SBLim-2A and SBLim-2M remain in service with the Polish Air Force.

MiG-15UTI-LL

There were a number of MiG-15UTI trainers converted for use as test beds. These aircraft were called MiG-15UTI-LL (LL, *Letajushtshaja laboratorija*, Flying laboratory). There were a number of MiG-15UTI-LLs used for ejection seat trials or for setting parachute records. Usually, for record attempts, the canopy was removed and the jumper was ejected from the aircraft.

Depending on the test program, either the front or the rear compartment was converted. The modified Mig-15UTIs were used in the Soviet Union for a number of trials using new ejection seat designs and an experimental escape capsule which was ejected with the pilot in it.

A Soviet MiG-15UTI Midget, Red 54, on final approach for landing. The tactical number is Red with a thin Black outline. The Midget was initially referred to as the UMiG-15 in service and operational manuals, but this designation was later changed to MiG-15UTI.

The MiG-15UTI Midget was named by its pilots as the *Babushka* (Grandmother) and *Matushka* (Good old Woman). The aircraft's armament consisted of a single UBK-E 12.7MM machine gun for gunnery training.

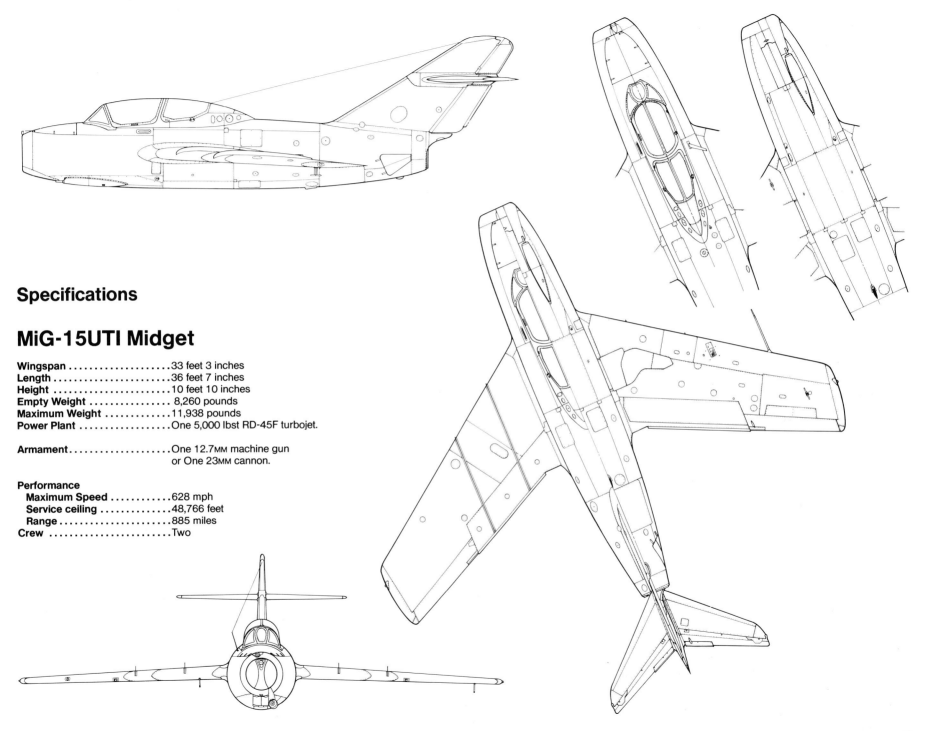

Specifications

MiG-15UTI Midget

Wingspan . . . . 33 feet 3 inches
Length . . . . 36 feet 7 inches
Height . . . . 10 feet 10 inches
Empty Weight . . . . 8,260 pounds
Maximum Weight . . . . 11,938 pounds
Power Plant . . . . One 5,000 lbst RD-45F turbojet.

Armament . . . . One 12.7мм machine gun
or One 23мм cannon.

Performance
  Maximum Speed . . . . 628 mph
  Service ceiling . . . . 48,766 feet
  Range . . . . 885 miles
Crew . . . . Two

A number of MiG-15UTIs were also converted for test bed use in various WARSAW Pact countries. In Poland several MiG-15UTIs were used for ejection seat trials. In another series of tests, the nose section of the PZL I-22 trainer was mounted above a MiG-15UTI (Red 002) for flight trials of the new design. Additionally, trials were conducted to investigate the ejection characteristics of the I-22. A Czech-built VS1-BRI ejection seat was installed in the mock up and a dummy was ejected from the I-22 while the MiG-15UTI performed a high speed taxi run.

Similar ejection seat tests were also performed in Czechoslovakia. One CS-102 was converted to accommodate the Czech developed VS-1BRI ejection seat. The rear canopy was deleted and the rear canopy frame was modified to accommodate the seat. The VS-1BRI ejection seat was intended for use in the Aero L-39 Albatros trainer. During one of the ejection trials, the MiG-15UTI test bed crashed, killing test pilot Rudolf Duchon. A second MiG-15UTI was modified in the same way and by 1977 some 115 ejections had been carried out by the MiG-15UTI test beds.

MiG-15UTI ST-7

The ST-7 was developed as a radar trainer to train pilots in the RP-1 *Izumrud-1* radar system. The ST-7 was unarmed, but carried an S-13 gun camera on the starboard side of the nose. The nose was converted in a similar manner to the MiG-15 SP-5 prototype to house the RP-1 radar system. To save weight most of aircraft's armor was deleted and the cockpit was redesigned to accommodate the additional radar associated equipment. In the event, the ST-7 was not produced in great numbers, since it was felt that the basic MiG-15UTI was sufficient for training. Once the pilot had transitioned into the MiG-17PF he could learn the radar techniques on training flights without the assistance of an onboard instructor.

UTI MiG-15P

During 1959, the Czech Air Force converted a CS-102 training aircraft as a radar trainer to instruct young pilots on the RP-5 *Izumrud-5* radar system which was being introduced on the MiG-17PF all weather fighter. The MiG-17PF was in the process of being delivered to the Czech Air Force.

The nose of the CS-102 was modified with the nose section of a MiG-19S Farmer, the RP-5 radar installation of a MiG-17PF and a tear dropped gun fairing on the port side of the nose (although often no gun was actually carried). Unlike the standard CS-102, the aircraft, designated the UTIMiG-15P in Czech service, did not carry an IFF antenna on the upper fuselage spine and the S-13 gun camera was not fitted.

There was only one UTIMiG-15P built and after completing its assigned training task, the aircraft was delivered to Praha-Kbely airfield where it is now on permanent display. Initially, the UTIMiG-15P was flown with 300 liter slipper tanks, which were later replaced by two 400 liter drop tanks. Late in its operational life, the aircraft reportedly had the tip of the tail painted in Gloss Blue.

A MiG-15UTI is readied for an early morning mission from its pierced steel plank (PSP) hardstand. The PSP system had been developed by the Americans and used for improvised airstrips in Eastern Europe. The aircraft's tactical number, Red 16, is repeated in White on the wheel chock.

This MiG-15UTI, Red 18, was assigned to Volunteer Society to Support the Army, Aviation and the Fleet (DOSAAF). This paramilitary organization used Air Force aircraft with the legend DOSSAF carried on the fuselage.

A pair of Finnish Air Force MiG-15UTI Midgets conduct formation training. MU-1 carries a 66 gallon (250 liter) slipper tank, with a painted tail, while MU-2 carries a 79 gallon (300 liter) tank. Finland operated a total of four MiG-15UTIs.

Polish ground crew load a battery for the R-800 radio set into the front equipment bay of this MiG-15UTI. The tactical number, Red 01, is rather weathered.

Rear cockpit of the MiG-15UTI Midget has the same instrumentation as the single-seat MiG-15 Fagot A fighter, but lacks a gun sight. Both cockpits are pressurized and separated by a large glass panel.

A MiG-15UTI Midget of the Indonesian Air Force (TNI-AU) during the 1960s. The tactical number J-762 was in Black. The aircraft in the background are MiG-17 Frescos and the Midget was used as a lead-in trainer for the Fresco.

A ground crewman refuels the 158.5 gallon (600 liter) drop tank on a Czech Air Force CS-102 (MiG-15UTI). Compared with the MiG-15bis the MiG-15UTI had a limited fuel capacity and wing tanks were normally carried.

An Albanian Air Force ground crew works on MiG-15UTI, Red 11, while dressed in Type L-2 chemical warfare suits during an exercise held in the early 1960s. The mechanic on the wing root is working on the ARK-5 compass which is accessible through the open access panel.

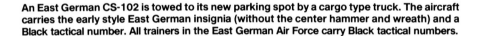

An East German CS-102 is towed to its new parking spot by a cargo type truck. The aircraft carries the early style East German insignia (without the center hammer and wreath) and a Black tactical number. All trainers in the East German Air Force carry Black tactical numbers.

An SBLim-2M assigned to the 45th Ground Attack Training Regiment based at Babimost during the Summer of 1990. Red 117 is overall White with a Yellow fin tip, identifying the aircraft as being assigned to the second squadron in the regiment.

A student pilot boards a Czech CS-102, Red 06, at the Officers School at Deblin, Poland. This CS-102 carries an improved fairing over the 12.7мм machine gun with a larger casing ejection port. Most of the Midgets used in Poland came from Czech production.

Fire fighters assist a pilot from an East German MiG-15 UTI during a training exercise. Late in their careers a number of East German Midgets were repainted in a camouflage paint scheme.

Armament Variations

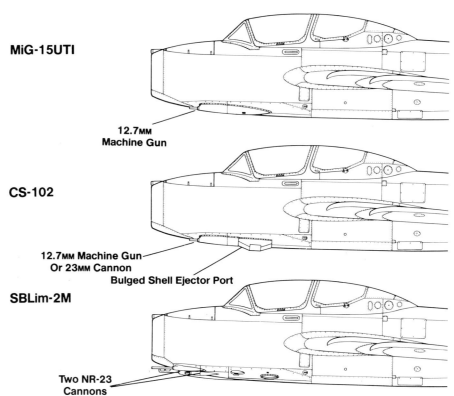

MiG-15UTI

12.7мм
Machine Gun

CS-102

12.7мм Machine Gun
Or 23мм Cannon

Bulged Shell Ejector Port

SBLim-2M

Two NR-23
Cannons

An overall Light Gray SBLim-2M, Red 319, plugged into a starter cart on a Polish Air Force base. The aircraft has a Yellow fin tip for the second squadron and has two NR-23 cannons in place of the 12.7мм machine gun carried on the SBLim-1.

This SBLim-1, Red 002, was used as a test-bed for the PZL I-22 jet trainer. A complete nose section of the I-22 was suspended above the Midget for ejection seat tests. The seat was ejected during high speed taxi to determine pilot survivability. The tail of the Midget was Yellow.

This CS-102 was used as an ejection seat test bed for Czech manufactured VS1-BRI ejection seats, which were to be used in the Aero L-39 Albatros. The rear canopy was removed and the canopy fairing was modified to accommodate the seat. The symbols on the tail denote successful ejections. The tests lasted until 1977.

A successful ejection seat test conducted from the rear cockpit of a Polish Air Force SBLim-2, Red 1018. The aircraft has had the rear canopy removed for the tests.

The ST-7 was developed as a radar systems trainer for the RP-1 *Izumrud-1* radar system. The S-13 gun camera was relocated to the starboard side of the nose and there is a cutout in the inboard wing fence.

The Czech built UTI-MIG-15P had a MiG-19 nose section with the radar from a MiG-17PF Fresco D. The aircraft was used as a crew trainer for pilots going into MiG-17PF squadrons. The lip above the air intake and the radome were in Light Blue. The UTI-MiG-15P is now on display at the Czech Aviation Museum in Kbely.

This Polish Air Force SBLim-2M reveals that tensions in the East have eased considerably. Not that many years ago, such light hearted markings would never have been permitted on a WARSAW Pact aircraft.

This ex-Polish Air Force Lim-2R (MiG-15R) (Serial 1B-01-420) was imported into England by Aces High Limited (registered as G-BMZF) The aircraft was used as a back drop for a Pilot's Pal photo session with model Susan Jane Watts during February of 1987. (Joe Marchant/Pilot's Pals).

This ex-Chinese Navy MiG-15bis (J-2, Serial 1411) was acquired by Combat Jets Inc. of Houston, Texas. The aircraft received an American registration N15MG and the Chinese markings were retained on the wings. White 4115 is active in flying air shows usually teamed with an F-86 Sabre.

Civil MiG-15s

This ex-Polish SBLim-2 (Serial 1A-06-038) was originally built as a Lim-1 fighter, then converted to the two seat configuration. The aircraft was imported to the U.S. and was used by the Defense Test and Evaluation Agency (civil contract) at Kirkland Air Force Base, New Mexico.

This Lim-2 (Serial 1B-01-205) was repainted in inaccurate Iraqi Air Force markings for the TV movie "Steal the Sky." The fuselage insignia is too large and in the wrong position and the fin flash is oversized. The aircraft has the civil registration N205JM.